# Chesapeake's Bounty II

Katie Moose

Conduit Press
Easton, MD

Front cover design: Jean Harper Baer, Baltimore, Maryland


Copyright ©2004   Conduit Press
2$^{nd}$ printing 2007

Published by Conduit Press, 111 Conduit Street, Annapolis, Maryland 21401.

Library of Congress Cataloging-in-Publication Data

Printed and Bound by Victor Graphics, Inc., Baltimore, Maryland, USA


ISBN: 0-9666610-7-9

# TABLE OF CONTENTS

## PICTURES

# INTRODUCTION

"Harmony Hills"

*"It is good food and not fine words that keeps me alive."*
Moliere (1622?-1673)

The Chesapeake Bay offers some of the finest seafood and produce in the world. Unfortunately pollution and disease have harmed the Bay, but even so its bounty has served many generations, including my ancestors who settled in Maryland in the 1600s. Just after World War II my Kennedy grandparents bought "Harmony Hills" farm, built in 1810 in Darlington. Over the years my grandfather had served three times at Aberdeen Proving Grounds. Not long after moving into the farm my parents moved to "Mount Pleasant" in Havre de Grace. It was there that I spent the first year of my life and Mrs. Bryan, owner of "Mount Pleasant" became my godmother. Over the years we returned to 'Harmony Hills" for day trips, holidays and special family occasions. If the dining room table overflowed we young ones were sent to the guest bedroom to eat our meals. The first time I remember eating artichokes was in that room. However most of the time we were privileged to eat in the dining room, served by Azzie, my grandmother's trusted cook. The farm is now a prominent horse breeding farm.

Today I enjoy the bounty while residing in the historic city of Easton on Maryland's Eastern Shore. But my ties are also to Delaware where I spent 9 years in New Castle and later to Alexandria, Virginia where my daughter was born. Over the years I developed a love of good food, good wine and learning to cook many international dishes as president of the International Visitor Centers in Cleveland and Newport.

This is my third cookbook. Each has a different feel, but each includes old family recipes, new creations and some shared by friends. The recipes are easy, but elegant. Even the most helpless cook can prepare anything from a cocktail party to Sunday brunch to a five or six course dinner. Enjoy the bounty of the Bay.

# HISTORICAL FACTS ON THE CHESAPEAKE BAY REGION

Chesapeake Bay Skipjacks

*"He who works not, eats not."*
*Captain John Smith of the Jamestown colony*

The first humans settled in the Chesapeake Bay region starting in about 10,000 BC. By 1500 BC they were known to have fed on oysters and in 1000 BC Native Americans begin making pottery. It was not until about 800 AD that native plants were grown and bow and arrows used for hunting. Shortly after that time the first permanent settlements were made by Native Americans. Until then they had wandered, traveling where they could find food.

The first European explorers came to the Chesapeake Bay region beginning with John Cabot who sailed off the Eastern Shore in 1498. In 1524 Giovanni de Verrazano entered the entrance to the Chesapeake Bay. Thomas Harriott published <u>A Brief and True Report of the New Found Land of Virginia</u> in London in 1588.

Jamestown was the first permanent English settlement in 1607. The settlers lived mainly on fish such as sturgeon and turtles. William Strachey wrote that "Tortoyses here (such as in the Bermudas) I have seene about the entrance of our bay, but we have not taken of them, but of the land tortoises we take and eate dailie…" They also ate animals they found nearby and some of the provisions they brought from Europe such as beef and pork that had probably been salted and smoked, or was brought over as livestock. The Native Americans shared corn, pumpkin, peppers, and squash with them, and they were able to pick berries. However between 1609-11 about half of the population died from starvation. Most of the original settlers were men. It was not until 1619 that a ship with 90 "young maids to make wives" arrived in Jamestown.

In 1608-09 John Smith began to explore and map the Chesapeake Bay. In 1612 John Rolfe of Jamestown, later husband of Pocohantas, discovered a type of tobacco from the West Indies that would grow well in Virginia. This provided the settlers with a cash crop.

In 1618 Virginians were asked to observe the Sabbath. On that day they could not work, play cards, dance, hunt, or fish. Even in 1622 public whippings in Virginia kept people from harvesting corn before it was ripe.

The earliest settlement in Delaware was in Lewes in 1631. Three years later the Ark and Dove arrive in St. Clement's, Maryland. St. Mary's City became the first permanent settlement and later the capital.

The Wye Mill, Wye Mills, Maryland dates from c1682 and is probably the oldest building still standing in the state. The mill has served as the boundary between Talbot and Queen Anne's Counties since 1706. In 1706 Richard Sweatman operated a sawmill and two gristmills here. Edward Lloyd controlled the mill from 1722 to 1793. Col. William Hemsley operated the mill for Mr. Lloyd and eventually owned it, having married Maria Lloyd, daughter of Edward Lloyd IV. The mill produced cornmeal for Gen. Washington's Continental Army at Valley Forge in 1778. The flour was ordered and paid for by Robert Morris. Alexander Hemsley sold the property to Samuel Hopkins in 1821 for $4,000. The state of Maryland eventually bought the mill. It was deeded to the Friends of Wye Mill in 1996. There is only one gristmill operating today still producing meal and flour.

In 1670 the Maryland governor restricted voting to planters with 50 acre freehold or property worth 40 pounds. Office holders had to own 1,000 or more acres.

The first market house opened in Wilmington, Delaware in 1736 and in 1742 Oliver Canby built the first flour mill on the Brandywine River. Eventually 130 mills would be located in the region, powered by the rushing river.

George Washington edited the Rules of Civility in 1744. This was to become the Emily Post of etiquette for that time.

In 1750 John Stevenson began shipping flour to Ireland from Baltimore, marking Baltimore as a trading city and major port. But by 1769 Maryland could no longer import British goods. Even so the Ellicott brothers founded the largest flour mill in Maryland on the Patapsco River in 1772. Corn, bread and rye were shipped from Baltimore to Boston. After the American Revolutionary War, John O'Donnell opened up trade from Baltimore with China.

Oliver Evans built the first automatic flour mill in Newport, Delaware in 1785. He granted a license to use his mill improvements to Thomas Jefferson in 1808. Mills were mainly powered by water. In 1822 Issac McKim milled flour for the first time in the United States with steam power.

As oystering and crabbing became major industries on the Bay several events allowed seafood and produce to be shipped to more faraway places. Thomas Kensett began the canning oysters in Baltimore in 1826 and in 1827 the ice box was invented. The opening of the Chesapeake and Delaware Canal in 1829 allowed boats to more easily access the Chesapeake Bay, instead of having to come in or out at the southern end. By the 1830s railroads were built and food could be transported to other parts of the country. During this time the iron range was invented for the kitchen. Now meals could be cooked on a stove or in an oven, rather than a kitchen hearth.

The first peach orchard was planted in Delaware in 1831. Eventually the state would produce thousands of bushels a year, earning it the nickname of the "Peach State".

Oystering on the Bay brought feuds between Maryland and Virginia who each claimed their own territories. In 1865 the Maryland General Assembly permitted oyster dredging, but only under sail as even then the oyster population was thinning. By 1868 Maryland authorized oyster police authorized to protect its boundaries. From 1888-89 Maryland and Virginia watermen fought oyster wars to stake out territories. In 1966 Maryland's oyster law permitted dredging under power 2 days a week

Farmers Markets are found throughout the Chesapeake Bay region. Some are only open weekends, others on a daily basis during the summer. Among the oldest is the Market Place in Annapolis which was designated the official market site in 1752.

The Virginia Beach Farmers Market opened in 1976. The original market began in Norfolk in the 17th c. This was burned by the British in 1776 and rebuilt in 1782. Once again the British burned it. Around 1900 one was built of brick. The market was moved several times before settling in its present location on Dam Neck Road. Newport News also sponsors a large farmer's market.

For exhibits on oystering and crabbing visit the Chesapeake Bay Maritime Museum in St. Michael's and the Oyster and Maritime Museum in Chincoteague. Other museums devoted to the Chesapeake Bay region are Havre de Grace Maritime Museum, the Decoy Museum in Havre de Grace; the Ward Museum in Salisbury, Maryland; the Agricultural Museum in Dover, Delaware; the Maritime Museum in Virginia Beach; the Maritime Museum in Annapolis; the Calvert Museum in Solomons; and the Reedville Fishermen's Museum.

# FESTIVALS

*"We gather together to ask the Lord's Blessing."*

Festivals have been around for hundreds of years. They are a time to celebrate a harvest, or in earlier times the planting, a time to bring a community together or to allow outsiders to join in the bounty of the land and Bay. Today they offer not only food, but music, crafts, beauty pageants, local customs and the sharing of recipes. Among the more popular festivals are:

J. Millard Tawes Crab and Clam Bake – Crisfield, Maryland - August
Shad roe – Wakefield Ruritan Club Shad Planking – Wakefield, Virginia - April
Seafood – Chincoteague – May and September or October
Belle Isle State Park, Virginia Bay Seafood Festival - September
Eastern Shore Harvest Festival, Virginia - October
Northern Neck Seafood Seafood Extravaganza, Ingleside – October
Colonial Beach, Virginia Lion's Club Oyster Roast - November
Poquoson Seafood Festival – Poquoson –October
River City Beer & Seafood Festival – Richmond - July
Bay Seafood Festival, Kilmarnock - September
Pungo Strawberry Festival, Virginia Beach – May
Fish Fries – King William Ruritan Club Fish Fry, King William, VA - April
Pork, Peanut and Pine Festival – Chippokes Plantation State Park, Surry, Virginia – July
Suffolk Peanut Festival – October
Urbanna Oyster Festival – November
Coast Day – University of Delaware, Lewes - October – seafood, chowder cook-off
Seafood Festival – Sandy Point State Park, Annapolis, MD – September – crab soup cook-off
Annapolis Rotary Crab Feast – August or September

# HISTORIC TAVERNS AND OTHER BUILDINGS

Gadsby's Tavern, Alexandria, Virginia was built as a tavern c 1785. John Gadsby operated it from 1796-1808. Many meetings, dances, musical performances and theatre took place here. Among the attendees were George Washington, John Adams, Thomas Jefferson, James Madison and Marquis de Lafayette.

Historic London Town and Gardens, Edgewater, Maryland was built in 1760 for William Brown, a cabinet maker and planter who also ran the ferry across the South River and a tavern (1752-1780s). London Town was a tobacco port on the South River beginning in the 17th c, and was considered as a site for the capital of Maryland. With recent excavations the site was discovered to date back hundreds of years earlier, having been settled by Native Americans of the Woodland Period (AD800-1600). The peninsula was used to harvest oysters, which were preserved by drying in the sun.

Nearby is the South River Club built in 1742 and is thought to be oldest social club in continuous use. Gentlemen met here every two weeks for dinner. The silver punchbowl has been in use since 1746. Today the club has 25 members who meet four times a year for a traditional Maryland dinner.

In 1653-54 Giles Brent received patents for 1800 acres called Piscataway Neck in Virginia. In 1739 the property passed to William Clifton who renamed the property Clifton's Neck. There he operated a ferry and inn. He ran into financial problems and the property was bought by George Washington of adjacent Mount Vernon. He changed the name to River Farm. Today the remaining house and a few acres are the headquarters for the American Horticultural Society.

Historic Williamsburg not only provides tours of its grounds but demonstrates 18th c cooking demonstrations and hog butchering, proper table settings at the Governor's Palace, and grows its own herbs and vegetables. The taverns and inns also serve authentic food. Shields Tavern in Williamsburg opened in 1988. It is named for James Shields who owned a tavern there in the 1740s. The tavern serves 18th c style food. Along the James River many of the plantations are still working farms.

The Gloucester Museum of History in Gloucester, Virginia was originally an 18th c ordinary tavern.

The Middlesex County Museum in Saluda, Virginia was originally a country store.

In Maryland working farms include Colonial Farm, Accokeek and Historic St. Mary's City.

The Kent Manor Inn, Stevensville, Maryland sits on a 226 acre tract once called Smithfield, which included "The Courthouse", now "Wetherell" granted to Thomas Wetherell in 1651. The left wing was constructed in 1820 and the center section just prior to the Civil War.

Rawlings' Tavern, Harwood, Maryland was owned by Jonathan Rawlings who was given a license to keep an "ordinary" in 1771. George Washington stopped here on his way to the Annapolis horse races in 1773.

The White Swan Tavern, Chestertown, Maryland was built in 1733 and became a tavern in 1793. Joseph Nicholson, whose two sons were famous naval officers during the Revolutionary War, operated the tavern.

The Kitty Knight House is the only house in Georgetown and Fredericktown, Maryland not burned by the British under Adm. Cockburn during War of 1812 when the owner refused to leave an elderly neighbor, and the British saved both homes.

The Blue Max Inn, Chesapeake City, Maryland was built c. 1854 for William Lindsey House and was once owned by Jack Hunter who wrote the novel, "The Blue Max".

The Bayard House, Chesapeake City, has won first place in the vegetable crab soup category at the Maryland Seafood Festival. The building dates c 1835.

# CHESAPEAKE BAY REGION WINERIES

Delaware, Maryland and Virginia have grown grapes since colonial times. But only recently have they received some recognition.

*Maryland*

Gov. Calvert of Maryland brought vines from France in 1662 and planted them on 200 acres. His best grape was called the "Alexander".

In 1942 Philip Wagner opened Boordy Vineyards in Maryland. He was an editorial columnist with the Baltimore Sun and went on to write the book "American Wines and How to Make Them" and "Grapes into Wine".

Today Maryland produces about 450 tons of grapes, about 300,000 bottles of wine. Wineries include Fiore Winery, Pykesville; Elk Run Vineyard and Winery, Mount Airy; Boordy Vineyard, Hydes; Basignani Winery, Sparks; Little Ashby Vineyards, Easton; and Woodhall Wine Cellars, Parkton.

*Virginia*

Wines were believed to have been produced as early as 1609. In 1773 Thomas Jefferson raised Italian grapes and designed his own wine cooler, which is on display at Monticello.

Virginia Wineries near the Chesapeake include Bloxom, Bloxom; Cooper, Louisa; Grayhaven, Gum Spring; Hummel, Montrose; James River Cellars, Glen Allen; Oak Crest, Dahlgren; The Williamsburg Winery, Williamsburg; and Ingleside Plantation Vineyards, Oak Grove.

*Delaware*

One of the grapes grown in the United States is known as the Delaware grape. This labrusca or table wine has low acidity and is somewhat bitter. However, the wine is not grown in Delaware, but Ohio!

The Delaware wineries include Nassau Valley Vineyards, Nassau and Felton Crest, Felton.

# APPETIZERS

Table Set for an Elegant Cocktail Party

Crab, oysters, fresh vegetables, and peanuts are used in traditional Chesapeake appetizers.

Peanuts were brought from Africa along with the slaves in the southern states. They were originally called groundnuts or ground peas and were used to feed pigs. During the Civil War soldiers ate the peanuts. Towards the end of the 1800s they were roasted and sold at PT Barnum's Circus. By 1900 equipment was developed to harvest and pick peanuts. Now they could be roasted or salted, made into peanut butter, candy, and used in peanut oil. Peanuts were first commercially grown in Virginia in the 1840s in Waverly, Sussex County. Waverly is now home to the first peanut museum in the US. Today over 250 million pounds are harvested on about 3,000 peanut farms. This is just less than 10% of the peanuts grown in the United States.

# CRAB SPRING ROLLS

1 Tbls sesame oil
2 cloves garlic, minced
1 jalapeno, seeded and minced
½ pound bean sprouts
½ pound carrots, shredded
½ red bell pepper, seeded, minced
2 Tbls. cilantro, chopped

2 Tbls. fresh ginger, grated
2 Tbls. dry sherry or rice wine
2 Tbls.soy sauce
1 pound fresh crab meat
Spring roll wrappers
1 small egg beaten
Vegetable oil

- ◆ Heat the oil in a wok. Add the garlic and jalapeno. Stir in the bean sprouts, carrot, pepper, cilantro, ginger, sherry and soy sauce.
- ◆ Remove from heat and stir in crab and salt and pepper.
- ◆ Place some of the filling on each spring roll wrapper. Fold over the top edges and the sides and seal the edges with the beaten egg.
- ◆ Heat the oil in the wok and fry spring rolls, a few at a time, until browned on all sides.
- ◆ Serve immediately, or keep warm in a 200° oven.
- ◆ Serve with hot mustard or soy sauce.

# CRAB BALLS

Makes 16 small crab balls

| | |
|---|---|
| 1 pound crab meat | 1 teaspoon Dijon mustard |
| 2 tablespoons bread crumbs | 2 tablespoons mayonnaise |
| 1 egg | Dash of Old Bay Seasoning |
| 1 teaspoon Worcestershire | Butter |

- ◆ With a fork carefully combine the ingredients in a bowl.  Shape into small cakes.
- ◆ Saute in butter until brown on each side.
- ◆ Serve on rounds cut out with a cookie cutter or small rimmed glass.
- ◆ Serve with green tomato relish – p. 199

# FRIED CRAB BALLS

| | |
|---|---|
| 1 pound crab meat | 2 Tbls. parsley, chopped |
| 2 tablespoons bread crumbs | 1 teaspoon dry mustard |
| 1 egg | ¼ cup red bell pepper, chopped |
| 1 teaspoon Worcestershire | 1 cup panko (Japanese bread |
| 2 tablespoons mayonnaise | crumbs) |
| Dash of Old Bay Seasoning | Vegetable oil |
| 1 green onion, chopped | |

- ◆ With a fork carefully combine the ingredients, except panko and oil in a bowl.  Shape into small balls.
- ◆ Coat the balls with the panko
- ◆ Heat the oil in a skillet. Drop the balls in and just brown. Serve with Green Sauce

*Green Sauce*

| | |
|---|---|
| ¼ cup mayonnaise | 2 Tbls. parsley, chopped |
| ¼ cup sour cream | 1 green onion, chopped |
| 2 Tbls. basil, chopped | |

- ◆ Combine ingredients in a bowl.

# HOT CRAB DIP

½ pound crab meat
8 oz. cream cheese
4 chives, snipped
½ cup sour cream

1 Tbls. Old Bay or Wye River Seasoning
1 teaspoon Worcestershire Sauce
½ cup slivered almonds

- Preheat oven to 350°
- Combine all ingredients, except almonds in a bowl. Place in shallow baking dish. Top with almonds.
- Bake 15 minutes or until bubbling.
- Serve with crackers, vegetables or toasted French bread slices.

# CRAB FLORENTINE DIP

2 Tbls. butter
½ pound fresh spinach
1 pound fresh crab meat

½ cup fresh basil, chopped
1 cup cream
½ cup parmesan cheese

- Preheat oven to 350°.
- In a skillet melt the butter and sauté the spinach until just wilted. Add more butter if needed.
- In a small low casserole put the spinach on the bottom.
- Top with crab and basil. Pour the cream over the crab. Sprinkle the parmesan cheese on top.
- Bake for 15 minutes or until just bubbling.
- Serve with thin sliced toasted French bread.

# CRAB DIP

1 pound crab meat
8 ounces cream cheese
½ pound cheddar cheese, grated
½ cup sour cream
¼ cup mayonnaise

¼ teaspoon Tabasco
1 teaspoon Old Bay Seasoning
or Wye River seasoning
3 chives, snipped

- ◆ Preheat oven to 350°
- ◆ Combine all the ingredients in a bowl. Pour into small baking dish. Bake for 15-20 minutes or until just bubbling browned.
- ◆ Serve with toasted French bread slices.

# CRAB DIP

1 pound crab meat
½ cup mayonnaise
½ cup sour cream
4 chives, snipped

1 can sliced water chestnuts
1 round loaf unsliced bread
2 cloves garlic, cut in half

- ◆ Preheat oven to 400°
- ◆ Combine ingredients, except bread and garlic in a bowl.
- ◆ Hollow out a round loaf of bread, saving bread cubes.
- ◆ Place the bread cubes on a baking sheet. Rub with garlic.
- ◆ Bake for 12 minutes or until just slightly browned and crisp.
- ◆ Place the crab mixture in the bread bowl. Serve with bread cubes.
- ◆ Crab mixture can also be heated in a sauce pan and served warm with bread.

# CRAB STUFFED MUSHROOMS

½ pound crab meat          Basil leaves
1 pound mushroom caps      Parmesan cheese, grated

- ♦ Preheat oven to 400°
- ♦ Place a spoonful of crab meat in each mushroom cap. Pour the sauce over the crab. Top with parmesan cheese.
- ♦ Bake for 10 minutes or until just browned.
- ♦ Serve with a basil leaf garnish

*White Wine Sauce*

½ stick butter             2 Tbls. fresh basil, chopped
¼ cup flour                ¼ cup Chardonnay
1 cup cream

- ♦ Melt the butter in a sauce pan. Stir in cream. Add wine and basil.

# MUSHROOMS STUFFED WITH CRAB

1 pound small portabella       ¼ pound fresh baby spinach
mushrooms, stems removed       ¼ cup heavy cream
½ pound fresh crab meat        2 Tbls. fresh basil, chopped

- ♦ Preheat oven to 350°.
- ♦ In a bowl combine the crab, spinach, cream and basil.
- ♦ Stuff the mushroom caps with the crab mixture.
- ♦ Bake in oven for 15 minutes or until bubbly.
- ♦ Artichoke hearts can be substituted for the spinach.

# STUFFED MUSHROOMS

2 green onions, chopped
¼ cup fresh basil, chopped
2 Tbls. fresh parsley, chopped
½ yellow bell pepper, chopped
1 teaspoon dry mustard

½ cup Monterey Jack cheese, grated
½ pound fresh crab meat
3 dozen mushroom caps

- ♦ Preheat oven to 350°
- ♦ Combine all the ingredients, except mushrooms in a bowl.
- ♦ Place the mushrooms on a baking tray. Stuff the caps with the crab meat mixture.
- ♦ Bake 15 minutes or until bubbling.

# STUFFED CHERRY TOMATOES

½ pound fresh crab meat
½ cup mayonnaise
¼ cup fresh parsley, chopped
1 teaspoon Old Bay or Wye River seasoning

¼ teaspoon paprika
½ teaspoon curry
2 Tbls. lemon juice
1 pint cherry tomatoes

- ♦ Combine all ingredients except tomatoes in a bowl.
- ♦ Cut the tomatoes in half.
- ♦ Place a spoonful of crab mixture on each tomato.

# CRAB CAKES WITH PEACH SALSA

1 pound crab meat
2 Tbls. fresh bread crumbs
1 egg
1 teaspoon Worcestershire sauce

1 teaspoon Dijon mustard
2 Tbls. mayonnaise
Dash of Old Bay seasoning
Butter

- In a bowl combine all the ingredients, except the butter. Make into small crab cakes.
- Melt the butter in a skillet. Saute the crab cakes until just browned.
- Place a round tray. Serve with the peach salsa.

*Peach Salsa*

2 large peaches, peeled, pitted and diced
2 jalapenos, seeded and chopped finely

2 Tbls. lime juice
2 Tbls. cilantro, chopped
1 scallion, finely chopped
1 Tbls. olive oil

- Combine all the ingredients in a bowl.

# CRAB WONTON

Wonton wrappers

½ pound crab
3 ounces cream cheese
2 Tbls. lemon juice

1 clove garlic, minced
2 green onions, chopped
Dash of Tabasco sauce

- Combine all the ingredients, except wonton wrappers in a bowl.
- Spread a spoonful of crab mixture on each wonton. Put a splash of water on each corner and fold opposite corners to the other.
- Fry in hot oil until just browned.
- Serve with hot mustard

# CLAMS WITH CRAB

18 clams in shell
½ pound crab meat
½ cup bread crumbs

¼ cup fresh basil, chopped
2 Tbls. lemon juice

- ◆ Preheat oven to 350°
- ◆ Place the clams on a baking sheet. Put in oven and cook until shells just open. Remove from oven. Open clams and remove one shell. Loosen clam.
- ◆ Combine the crab, crumbs, basil and lemon juice in a bowl. Spoon mixture over each clam. Pour either cheese or tomato sauce on top. Do not use both, unless you want some with each mixture.
- ◆ Bake for 15 minutes or until just bubbling.

*Cheese Sauce*

½ stick butter
¼ cup flour

1 cup half and half
½ cup Gruyere

- ◆ Melt butter in a sauce pan. Stir in butter and half and half until thickened. Add cheese.

*Tomato Sauce*

3 large tomatoes, chopped
¼ cup fresh basil, chopped

¼ cup olive oil
2 large closed garlic, minced

- ◆ Combine all ingredients in a sauce pan. Stir until tomatoes are very soft.

# CRAB BALLS WITH BASIL CREAM

*Crab Balls*

1 pound crab meat
2 Tbls. fresh bread crumbs
1 egg
1 teaspoon Worcestershire sauce

1 teaspoon Dijon mustard
2 Tbls. mayonnaise
Dash of Old Bay seasoning
Butter

- In a bowl combine all the ingredients, except the butter. Make into small balls.
- Melt the butter in a skillet. Saute the crab balls until just browned.
- Place on a tray and serve hot with the basil cream.

*Basil Cream*

½ stick butter
¼ cup flour

1 cup heavy cream
½ cup fresh basil, chopped

- In a sauce pan melt the butter. Stir in the flour and slowly stir in the cream.
- Stir in the basil.
- Instead of making crab cakes, stir just the crab meat into the basil cream. Serve as a dip with French bread, or over rice or pasta as a main dish.

# ENDIVE STUFFED WITH CRAB

½ pound crab meat
½ cup mayonnaise
2 Tbls. fresh basil, chopped

2 Tbls. lemon juice
½ pound endive leaves

- Combine the crab, mayonnaise, basil and lemon juice in a bowl.
- Stuff each endive leaf with the crab mixture.
- This is also good using snow peas.

# CRAB FRITTERS

1 cup flour
1 teaspoon baking powder
2 eggs
1 teaspoon salt

¼ teaspoon pepper
1 cup milk
1 pound fresh crab meat
Oil

- ◆ Combine the flour, baking powder, salt and pepper in a bowl.
- ◆ In another bowl beat together the eggs and milk. Stir in dry ingredients. Fold the crab into the mixture.
- ◆ Pour about 1 inch oil into a skillet. Heat until bubbly.
- ◆ Make the crab mixture into golf size balls.
- ◆ Fry in hot oil until just browned.
- ◆ Keep warm in oven.
- ◆ Serve with Tabasco sauce

*Tabasco sauce*

½ cup sour cream
3 chives, snipped

½ teaspoon Tabasco

- ◆ Combine ingredients in bowl.

# CRAB RAVIOLI

1 package won ton wrappers
1 pound crab meat
¼ cup fresh parsley, chopped

½ cup fresh grated Gruyere cheese
1 clove garlic, crushed
3 ½ cups water

- ◆ In a bowl combine the crab, parsley, cheese and garlic.
- ◆ Spoon one tablespoon of crab mixture on won ton wrapper, leaving a slight edge. Fold the won ton in half and seal with water.
- ◆ In a sauce pan bring the water to a boil. Drop in the wonton and cook for about six minutes.
- ◆ Serve with more grated cheese or a tomato sauce.

# OYSTERS MORNAY

Makes 48, or serves 4 as a main dish

4 dozen oysters in the shell
½ pound baby spinach
4 green onions, chopped
1 teaspoon nutmeg

1 pound of fresh crab meat
½ cup grated parmesan cheese
Paprika
Cilantro leaves

- ♦ Preheat oven to 350°
- ♦ Place the oysters on a baking sheet and bake in oven until shells just open. Remove from oven and remove top shell.
- ♦ Place some of the spinach, green onion, nutmeg and crab meat on top of each oyster.
- ♦ Top with Mornay sauce, parmesan cheese and paprika.
- ♦ Place under broiler until just slightly browned and bubbling.
- ♦ Serve on a platter and garnish with fresh cilantro leaves.

*Mornay Sauce*

½ stick butter
¼ cup flour
1½ cups half and half

1 teaspoon Dijon mustard
¼ cup fresh grated parmesan cheese

- ♦ Melt the butter in a sauce pan. Stir in the flour, then half and half until thickened. Stir in the parmesan cheese.

# FRIED OYSTERS

2 dozen fried oysters-p. 79
Jalapeno mayonnaise sauce

*Jalapeno Mayonnaise Sauce*

2 jalapeno peppers, seeded and chopped finely
½ cup mayonnaise

¼ cup cilantro, chopped
2 Tbls. lime juice

Combine ingredients in a bowl.

# STUFFED OYSTERS

24 oysters with shell
¼ cup fresh parsley, chopped
½ red bell pepper, chopped
1 stalk celery, chopped
¼ cup onion, chopped

4 strips bacon
1 tomato, chopped
¼ teaspoon cayenne
Juice of ½ lemon

- ♦ Preheat oven to 300°. Place the oysters in the oven until the shell opens.
- ♦ In a skillet cook the bacon. Remove and chop. Reserve the fat. Add the vegetables and cook until tender. Add the cayenne and lemon juice.
- ♦ Remove one shell from each oyster and top the oyster with the vegetable mixture. Broil until bubbling.

# OYSTERS ROCKEFELLER

1 stick butter
2 green onions, chopped
½ pound baby spinach
¼ cup fresh parsley, chopped
3 cloves garlic, minced

Juice of ½ lemon
½ teaspoon Tabasco or cayenne
24 oysters in shell
Bread crumbs

- ♦ Preheat oven to 350°
- ♦ Place oysters on a cookie sheet and cook in oven until oysters just open. Remove from oven. Cool. Remove top shell from oyster and discard.
- ♦ Melt the butter in a sauce pan. Add onions, and spinach. Just braise spinach. Add parsley, garlic, lemon juice and Tabasco. Spoon mixture over each oyster. Top with bread crumbs.
- ♦ Bake for 10 minutes, or until just browned.
- ♦ Serve warm.

# OYSTER BLINI

2 dozen shucked oysters with liquor

- ♦ Warm oysters in liquor in a sauce pan. Drain.
- ♦ Place each oyster on a blini. Top with a spoonful of the sauce.
- ♦ Crab meat can be substituted for the oysters.

*Blini*

| | |
|---|---|
| 1 cup flour | 1 egg |
| ½ cup buckwheat flour | 1 cup milk |
| ¼ cup sugar | ¼ cup sour cream |
| 1 Tbls. baking powder | 2 Tbls. melted butter |

- ♦ In a bowl beat all ingredients. Drop by small spoonful onto griddle. Cook 3-4 minutes each side until just browned.

*Horseradish Sauce*

| | |
|---|---|
| 1 cup sour cream | 2 chives, snipped |
| 2 Tbls. horseradish | Juice of 1 lemon |

- ♦ Combine ingredients in a bowl.

# MARINATED SHRIMP

Can also be used as a main course

| | |
|---|---|
| 1 pound large shrimp, cooked, peeled and deveined | ½ cup red pepper, chopped |
| | ½ cup yellow pepper, chopped |
| ½ cup lime juice | Kernels from 1 ear corn |
| 1 teaspoon sea salt | 3 green onions, chopped |
| ¼ cup olive oil | 1 jalapeno, chopped |
| ¼ cup cilantro, chopped | |

- ♦ Combine all ingredients in a bowl. Chill.
- ♦ Serve on a fish platter. Garnish with more cilantro.

# SMOKED SALMON BLINI

½ pound smoked salmon
20 medium shrimp, cooked peeled

2 large avocado, peeled, pitted and sliced thinly

- ♦ Place a small piece of salmon on each blini. Top with a shrimp and avocado slice. Spoon a small amount of horseradish sauce on top.
- ♦ Serve on fish plate.

*Blini*

1½ cups flour
¼ cup sugar
1 Tbls. baking powder
1 egg

1 cup milk
¼ cup sour cream
2 Tbls. melted butter

- ♦ In a bowl beat all ingredients. Drop by small spoonful onto griddle. Cook 3-4 minutes each side until just browned.

*Horseradish Cream*

½ cup sour cream
½ cup heavy cream
2 Tbls. horseradish

2 chives, chopped
Juice of 1 lemon

- ♦ Combine ingredients in a bowl.

# CHEESE ROLL

½ pound cheddar cheese
½ pound blue cheese
2½ cups flour

1 cup butter
1 cup pecans
1 teaspoon cayenne

- ♦ Place all ingredients in food processor. Blend until a ball is formed.
- ♦ Roll into a log. Wrap in foil and refrigerate overnight.
- ♦ When ready to serve, slice roll and bake 10 minutes at 300°.

# RISOTTO BALLS

1 Tbls. butter  
1 cup risotto  
1 ½ cups hot chicken stock  
2 Tbls. leeks, chopped

½ cup sun-dried tomato, chopped  
¼ cup basil, chopped

- ♦ Melt the butter in a sauce pan. Add risotto, leeks, tomato and basil and slowly add stock. Cook until risotto is tender, stirring constantly. About 20 minutes.
- ♦ Shape the risotto into golf size balls.
- ♦ Melt 2 Tbls. butter in a skillet. Brown the balls in the skillet. Add more butter if needed.
- ♦ Serve hot on a platter.
- ♦ ¼ pound portabello mushrooms, chopped, can be substituted for the sun-dried tomatoes and basil. Add ½ cup crumbled Gorgonzola cheese.

# MARINATED MUSHROOMS

1 pound mushrooms, sliced  
Juice of 1 lemon  
½ cup olive oil  
2 green onions, chopped  
¼ cup parsley, chopped

2 Tbls. fresh dill, chopped  
1 Tbls oregano, chopped  
½ teaspoon salt  
½ teaspoon pepper

- ♦ Combine all ingredients in a bowl. Marinate refrigerated overnight.

# CREPES WITH MUSHROOM FILLING

Serves 4

*Crepes* (p. 182)

- ◆ Preheat oven to 350°
- ◆ Along the center of each crepe spread some of the mushroom mixture. Fold crepe from each side and then at ends.
- ◆ Bake in oven for 15 minutes.
- ◆ Serve hot.

*Filling*

½ stick butter
¼ cup flour
1½ cups half and half
2 Tbls. Sherry

2 Tbls. butter
1 pound mushrooms, sliced
½ cup coconut

- ◆ Melt the butter in a sauce pan. Add flour and stir in half and half and Sherry.
- ◆ In a skillet lightly sauté mushrooms.
- ◆ Add mushrooms and coconut to sauce.
- ◆ Chicken or ham can be added for a hearty meal.

# MUSHROOM BRUSCHETTA

2 pounds grilled portabella mushrooms, chopped
Sage cream sauce (white wine sauce with 1 Tbls. sage added) – p. 208

1 loaf French bread, sliced and toasted

- ◆ Place a mushroom slice on each slice of bread. Top with sage cream sauce.

# STUFFED MUSHROOMS

1 pound large mushrooms such as portabella, wash and remove stems

½ pound Smithfield ham, ground up
½ cup parsley, chopped

- ♦ In a bowl combine the sauce, chopped mushroom stems, ham and parsley.
- ♦ Stuff mushrooms with mixture. Place on baking sheet.
- ♦ Bake in oven for 15 minutes or until bubbly.
- ♦ Serve on platter and garnish with fresh parsley.

*Bechamel Sauce*

½ stick butter
¼ cup flour
1 cup half and half

½ cup Gruyere cheese
2 Tbls. Sherry
½ teaspoon nutmeg

- ♦ Melt butter in a sauce pan. Stir in flour and half and half and half until thickened. Stir in cheese until melted. Add Sherry and nutmeg.

# MEATBALLS

1 pound ground beef
1 egg
½ cup bread crumbs
½ cup Monterey Jack cheese

2 green onions, chopped
2 jalapenos, chopped
salt and pepper

- ♦ Combine all ingredients in a bowl. Shape into small balls.
- ♦ Brown in olive oil in a skillet.
- ♦ Serve warm with salsa.

*Salsa*

2 large tomatoes, chopped
2 large cloves garlic, minced
1 Tbls. vinegar

2 Tbls. olive oil
¼ cup chopped cilantro
Juice of 1 lime

- ♦ Combine all ingredients in a bowl.

# MEAT PASTRIES

½ pound ground lamb
1 small onion, chopped
2 hard boiled eggs, chopped
½ cup raisins

2 Tbls. parsley, chopped
2 Tbls. dill, chopped
¼ teaspoon cayenne

- ◆ Preheat oven to 400°
- ◆ Cook beef and onion in a skillet until beef is just browned. Cool. Stir in rest of ingredients.
- ◆ Put pastries on ungreased cookie sheet.
- ◆ Place rounded teaspoon of mixture on a pastries. Fold pastry in half and seal with a little water.
- ◆ Bake 15-20 minutes or until golden brown.
- ◆ These can also be deep fried in oil.

*Pastry*

1 stick butter
2 cups flour

½ teaspoon salt
½ cup sour cream

In a food processor blend all ingredients. Roll out dough on a floured board. Use a large biscuit cutter (3" diameter)to make pastries.

# ASPARAGUS SANDWICHES

1 loaf thin white bread
1 pound thin asparagus, ends trimmed to fit on bread

8 oz. cream cheese, softened
1 stick melted butter
½ cup parmesan cheese

- ◆ Preheat oven to 400°
- ◆ Cut the crust off the bread. Spread the bread with a small layer of cream cheese. Place 1 asparagus on each slice. Roll up bread. Secure with a toothpick.
- ◆ Roll in butter and then cheese.
- ◆ Bake for 12 minutes or until just browned.
- ◆ Serve immediately.

# STUFFED EGGS

12 hard boiled eggs
¼ cup mayonnaise
Juice of 1lemon
1 teaspoon Dijon mustard

Dash of cayenne
2 Tbls. parsley, chopped
2 chives, snipped
½ pound fresh crab meat

- ◆ Slice the eggs in half. Remove yolk.
- ◆ In a bowl combine yolk, mayonnaise, lemon juice, mustard, cayenne, parsley, and chives.
- ◆ Stuff the eggs with the mixture.
- ◆ Top with a small amount of the crab.

# GORGONZOLA AND TOMATO BRUSCHETTA

½ cup olive oil
3 large cloves garlic, minced
4 large ripe tomatoes, finely
chopped

¼ cup fresh basil, finely
chopped
½ pound Gorgonzola cheese,
crumbled
1 loaf French bread

- ◆ Preheat broiler.
- ◆ Slice the French into ½" slices.
- ◆ In a bowl combine the olive oil, garlic, tomatoes and basil. Cover each slice of bread with the tomato mixture. Top with the crumbled cheese.
- ◆ Place under broiler until cheese is just bubbling.

# DEVILED EGGS

12 eggs
Juice of 1 lemon
½ stick butter, melted

2 Tbls. parsley, chopped
2 Tbls. watercress, chopped
Caviar

- ◆ Hard boil eggs. Peel under running water immediately.
- ◆ Cut bottoms off egg so they can sit. Cut eggs in half. Scoop yolks out.
- ◆ Combine yolks, lemon juice and butter in a bowl. Spoon into egg whites.
- ◆ Garnish with parsley, watercress or the caviar.

# GOUGERE

1 cup water
6 Tbls. butter
1 teaspoon salt

1 cup flour
4 eggs
½ pound Swiss Cheese, grated

- ◆ Preheat oven to 425°
- ◆ Combine the water, butter and salt in a sauce pan. Bring to a boil and butter melts.
- ◆ Stir in the flour until a ball is formed. Beat in the eggs, one at a time. Stir the cheese, except for 2 Tbls. into mixture.
- ◆ Drop by tablespoons onto greased cookie sheet in crown shape. Leave a hole in the center. Top with remaining cheese.
- ◆ Bake for 25 minutes or until well browned. Must be cooked through or it will collapse.
- ◆ Gruyere can be substituted for Swiss Cheese.

# CHICKEN LIVER PATE

½ stick butter
1 pound chicken livers
½ pound mushrooms
2 green onions, sliced
½ cup dry white wine

4 cloves garlic, minced
1 Tbls rosemary
2 Tbls. dill
¼ cup cognac

- ♦ Melt butter in skillet. Add chicken livers, mushrooms and onions. Cook for about 10 minutes, and livers are pink. Add wine.
- ♦ Place all ingredients in food processor.
- ♦ Serve with toasted French bread slices.

# SPICED PECANS

1 pound shelled pecans
1 teaspoon cumin
½ teaspoon cayenne
1 teaspoon chili powder

½ cup butter, melted
1 Tbls. kosher salt
¼ cup sugar

- ♦ Preheat oven to 300°
- ♦ Place the pecans on a baking sheet. Sprinkle the cumin, cayenne and chili powder on nuts. Toss to coat all nuts. Sprinkle salt and sugar on top.
- ♦ Bake 30 minutes. Be careful not to burn the nuts.
- ♦ Walnuts or other nuts can be substituted for pecans.

# CANDIED WALNUTS OR PECANS

1 egg white

1 Tbls. water

1 pound walnuts or pecans

½ cup sugar

1 teaspoon cinnamon

1/2 teaspoon salt

- ◆ Preheat oven to 300°
- ◆ In a bowl beat the egg white till stiff. Add water. Roll pecans in egg white, then cinnamon and salt.
- ◆ Bake for ½ hour.

# BELGIAN ENDIVE WITH CHEESE

Endive

Gorgonzola cheese

Toasted chopped walnuts or slivered almonds

- ◆ Stuff the endive with a small amount of the cheese and nuts.
- ◆ Serve on a platter.
- ◆ Snow peas can be substituted for the endive.

# SPECIAL DRINKS

In the early 50's we lived in New Castle, Delaware. My parents had a wonderful group of friends. They were young, most newly wed, and didn't have much money. They came up with the idea of a "Garbage Party". Bring your favorite leftover dishes. However everyone contributed something delicious. Many times the parties had a theme such as an upside party. They came up with some of the craziest costumes imaginable. As you can see from the picture these were the days of cigarettes and martinis, which my father is pouring. Happily pictures bring back many memories of a group of people that we all knew as "Aunt so and so" or "Uncle so and so". Sadly many of them have left us, but they are unforgettable.

Did you know Thomas Jefferson had an extensive wine cellar? Much of it was imported from Europe, though some have been made at Monticello.

George Washington also made whiskey at Mount Vernon. An exhibit on this was recently opened.

On October 19, 1774 Annapolis celebrated its own tea party when the *Peggy Stewart* loaded with British tea was burned in the harbor. Her owner, though from Annapolis, was a British sympathizer.

Just north of the Chesapeake Bay, Hires Root Beer was first produced by pharmacist Charles E. Hires in Philadelphia. The root beer is known as the original U.S. brand and is the oldest continuously marketed soft drink. His first brew was a tea comprised of roots, berries and herbs concocted on his honeymoon. The root beer was introduced at the 1876 US Centennial Exposition in Philadelphia. Today Hires is owned by Dr. Pepper/Seven Up.

The first public drinking fountain in Wilmington, Delaware appeared in 1870.

# ORANGE SHRUB

2 quarts fresh orange juice       1 bottle dark rum
2 cups sugar

- ♦ Combine all ingredients in a punch bowl.
- ♦ Place an ice wreath in bowl.
- ♦ Serve in punch glasses.

# RUM PUNCH

10 glasses

4 cups pineapple juice       Juice of 1 lime
4 cups orange juice       Dash of Angostura bitters
3 teaspoons Grenadine       Sliced limes
2 cups dark rum

- ♦ Combine all ingredients in a pitcher. Serve in tall glasses with ice.

# FROZEN DAIQUIRI

1 cup dark rum       ¼ cup sugar
1 cup light rum       1 tray ice cubes
2 cups lime juice

- ♦ Combine all ingredients in a blender. Serve immediately in martini or Marguerita glasses.

# STRAWBERRY DAIQUIRI

Serves 1

2 oz. dark rum
½ cup strawberries
½ oz. Triple Sec

1 Tbls. lime juice
½ cup crushed ice

♦ Place all ingredients in blender until smooth. Serve immediately.

# PEACH DAIQUIRI

1 serving

1 large ripe peach, peeled, pitted
and sliced
1 Tbls. lime juice

1 teaspoon sugar
3 oz. dark rum
4 ice cubes

♦ Combine all ingredients in a blender. Serve in a Margarita glass.

# RUM GIMLET

Serves 1

2 oz. rum
½ oz. Roses lime juice

Lime slice
Ice

♦ Place an ice cube in a martini glass. Pour the rum and lime juice
   into glass. Serve with lime slice.
♦ Gin can be substituted to make a gin gimlet.

# PINA COLADA

Serves 1

2 oz. rum
1 oz. coconut cream
1 oz. heavy cream

½ cup pineapple juice
½ cup crushed ice

♦ Combine all ingredients in a blender.  Pour into a tall glass.

# ICED COFFEE

Serves 1

1 cup strong coffee
1½ oz. dark rum

Whipped cream
Ice

♦ Put the ice cubes in a tall glass. Pour in the coffee and rum. Top
with the whipped cream.

# BLOODY MARY

For 6 drinks

32 oz. V 8 juice
2 Tbls. horseradish
Juice of ½ lime
½ teaspoon fresh ground pepper

1 cup bouillion
4 drops Tabasco
1 Tbls. Worcestershire sauce

♦ Combine all the ingredients in a pitcher. Serve over ice with
celery.

# SANGRIA

Makes 16 cups

2 cups orange juice
1 bottle ginger ale
2 bottles Burgundy

Lemon slices
Orange slices
Ice mold

♦ In a punch bowl combine the orange and burgundy. Pour in the ginger ale. Add orange and lemon slices and ice mold. Serve in punch cups.

# MINT JULEP

For 1 drink

1 teaspoon sugar
1 teaspoon water
6 mint leaves

4 oz. bourbon
Crushed ice

♦ In a glass crush 3 of the mint leaves with the sugar and water. Fill the glass with the ice. Pour the bourbon over the mixture.

# HOT MULLED CIDER

Makes 10 cups

2 quarts apple cider
½ cup brown sugar
1 teaspoon allspice
1 teaspoon ground cloves

1 teaspoon cinnamon
½ teaspoon nutmeg
2 cups orange juice
Orange slices

♦ Combine all the ingredients except orange slices in large pot. Bring to a boil. Simmer 10 minutes.
♦ Serve hot with orange slices.
♦ Rum can be added for a stronger drink.

# EGGNOG

Makes 24 cups

12 eggs separated
2 ¼ cups sugar
4 cups milk
4 cups bourbon or rum, or combination of both

4 cups heavy cream
Zest of 1 orange
Zest of 1 lemon
Nutmeg

- Beat the egg yolks. Add sugar and beat until pale yellow in color. Stir in milk and bourbon.
- Beat egg whites until firm in separate bowl. Fold into yolk mixture.
- Beat cream in bowl until peaks form. Fold into mixture.
- Serve in punch bowl. Sprinkle with nutmeg.

# WHISKEY SOUR

Juice of ½ large lemon
4 oz. bourbon
1 teaspoon sugar

4 ice cubes
1 maraschino cherry
1 orange slice

- Combine the lemon juice, bourbon and sugar in a glass. Add ice cubes. Finish with cherry and orange slice.

# ICED TEA

Serves 8

6 cups strong tea
½ teaspoon ground cloves
½ teaspoon cinnamon

¼ teaspoon nutmeg
2 cups lemonade
¼ cup honey

- Combine all the ingredients in a pitcher. Serve over ice in tall glasses and garnish with a lemon slice.

# SOUPS

Chesapeake Bay Crab Boat

*"Only the pure of heart can make good soup"*
Beethoven

The Campbell soup tureen collection at Winterthur Museum is one of the most extensive in the world. The tureens come in every shape from rabbits and other animals to extraordinarily elaborate gilded bowls. The museum, located outside Wilmington, Delaware, has over 170 rooms and magnificent gardens.

# CRAB SOUP

Serves 4

½ stick butter
2 carrots, sliced
1 medium onion, chopped
1 cup fresh lima beans or chopped green beans
4 cups chicken broth
4 tomatoes, chopped

4 potatoes, peeled and chopped
2 teaspoons Old Bay or Wye River seasoning
1 pound crab meat
¼ cup parsley or watercress, chopped

- ♦ Melt the butter in a large pot. Add carrots and onion. Cook for 5 minutes.
- ♦ Add rest of ingredients except for crab and parsley. Just heat. Add crab.
- ♦ Serve in bowls with parsley

# CRAB AND CORN CHOWDER

Serves 6

½ stick butter
2 cups fresh corn
1 small onion, chopped
6 red bliss potatoes, cubed
3 stalks celery, chopped

3 slices cooked bacon, crumbled
4 cups chicken stock
2 cups heavy cream
1½ pounds fresh crab meat
½ cup parsley, chopped

- ◆ Melt the butter in a large pot. Add the corn, potatoes, onion and celery. Saute for 5 minutes.
- ◆ Add chicken stock. Bring to a boil. Cook until potatoes are just tender.
- ◆ Stir in cream and crab. Just heat.
- ◆ Serve in bowls garnished with parsley.

# CRAB AND ASPARAGUS SOUP

Serves 4

½ stick butter
½ pound asparagus, chopped
½ cup leeks, chopped
3 cups chicken stock

1 cup heavy cream
1 pound crab meat
Watercress

- ◆ Melt the butter in a pot. Stir in asparagus and leeks until just tender.
- ◆ Add stock and cream. Stir in crab meat.
- ◆ Serve in bowls garnished with watercress.

# SPINACH CRAB WONTON SOUP

Serves 4

*Broth*

4 cups chicken broth
2 green onions, chopped

12 leaves baby spinach

- ◆ Heat the ingredients in a sauce pan to a boil. Drop in wonton for 2 minutes. Serve immediately.

*Wonton*

½ pound crab meat
1 Tbls. soy sauce
2 Tbls. Sherry
Wonton wrappers

1 green onion
½ can water chestnuts

- ◆ Combine the crab, soy sauce, Sherry, green onion and water chestnuts in a food processor.
- ◆ Spread a spoonful of the mixture on a wonton wrapper. Fold on diagonal and bring two ends together, sealing with water.

# CURRIED CRAB SOUP

Serves 6

1 small onion, chopped
2 tablespoons butter
¼ cup flour
1 quart cream or half and half
1 cup chicken stock
Cilantro leaves

Salt and pepper
1 Tbls. curry
½ teaspoon ginger
1 pound crab meat

- ◆ Saute the onion in butter until transparent. Stir in flour.
- ◆ Add the chicken stock and slowly pour in the cream until thickened. Add salt, pepper, curry and ginger. Fold in crab.
- ◆ Serve soup in bowls, garnished with cilantro.

# CRAB AND CORN BISQUE

Serves 8

| | |
|---|---|
| 1 stick butter | 2 scallions, chopped |
| ½ cup flour | 4 cups fresh corn |
| 4 cups light cream | 2 pounds crab meat |
| 4 cups heavy cream | Fresh basil leaves |

- ◆ In a large sauce pan melt the butter. Stir in the flour. Add the creams until slightly thickened.
- ◆ Add scallions, corn and crab.
- ◆ Pour into soup bowls. Garnish with basil leaves.

# CRAB AND SQUASH SOUP

Serves 4

| | |
|---|---|
| ½ stick butter | 1 cup cheddar cheese |
| 2 carrots, peeled and sliced | 2 cups heavy cream |
| 1 onion, chopped | 1 Tbls. curry |
| ¼ cup flour | Salt and pepper |
| 2 cups chicken stock | 1 pound crab meat |
| 1 pound butternut squash, peeled and diced | Cilantro |

- ◆ Melt the butter in a large pot. Add carrots and onion. Cook until onion is transparent.
- ◆ Stir in flour and chicken stock. Add squash and cheese. Cook for 5 minutes or until cheese is just melted.
- ◆ Add cream, curry and salt and pepper to taste. Fold in crab.
- ◆ Serve warm or chilled.
- ◆ Serve in bowls. Garnish with cilantro.

# OYSTER SOUP

Serves 4-6

½ stick butter
4 scallions, chopped
2 stalks celery, chopped
1 quart half and half

¼ pound Smithfield ham, chopped
1 quart oysters with liquor

- ◆ Melt the butter in a pot. Add scallions and celery and sauté. Stir in half and half and ham.
- ◆ Add oysters and liquor. Bring to a boil.
- ◆ Serve immediately with chopped parsley.
- ◆ For a thicker soup stir in ¼ cup flour before adding half and half.

# OYSTER SPINACH SOUP

Serves 4-6

½ stick butter
1 small onion, chopped
½ pound baby spinach
1 clove garlic, minced

¼ cup flour
3 cups half and half
1 cup chicken stock
1 quart oysters and liquor

- ◆ Melt the ¼ stick butter in a pot. Stir in onion until translucent. Add spinach and garlic. Place in food processor and puree.
- ◆ Melt rest of butter in pot.
- ◆ Stir in flour. Add half and half and chicken stock.
- ◆ Add spinach puree, oysters and liquor.
- ◆ Serve hot.

# OYSTER CHOWDER

Serves 4

1 quart oysters with liquor
4 strips bacon
4 red bliss potatoes, peeled and cubed
2 Tbls. shallots, minced

½ pound fresh spinach
2 Tbls. butter
1 quart heavy cream
½ teaspoon fresh ground pepper
½ cup white cheddar cheese

- Cook the potatoes in boiling water until tender. Drain
- In a large sauce pan cook the bacon until crispy. Remove and drain fat.
- Melt the butter in the skillet and saute shallots and spinach briefly.
- Add bacon, cream, oyster liquor, potato, and pepper. Bring to a boil.
- stir in cheddar cheese until melted. Add oysters and simmer for 5 minutes.
- Serve immediately. Garnish with fresh dill.

# OYSTER STEW

Serves 4-6

4 slices bacon
½ stick butter
1 small onion, chopped
4 red bliss potatoes, diced
2 cloves garlic, minced
3 Tbls. parsley
2 chives, snipped

4 cups half and half
1 quart shucked oysters with liquor
½ teaspoon salt
1 teaspoon fresh ground pepper
½ teaspoon thyme

- In a pot cook the bacon. Remove bacon and add butter, onion, and potatoes. Cook until vegetables are just tender.
- Add garlic, parsley, chives and half and half and liquor. Bring to a boil. Add oysters. Simmer for 5 minutes.
- Serve in a soup tureen or individual bowls with a pat of butter.

# ROCKFISH CHOWDER

Serves

4 large potatoes, peeled and cubed
½ pound bacon
½ stick butter
1 medium onions, chopped
4 cloves garlic, minced
½ cup parsley, chopped

4 bay leaves
2 pounds rockfish fillets
Salt, pepper
2 teaspoons thyme
2 quarts half and half
Sherry

- In a large pot boil the potatoes until just tender. Remove.
- Cut the bacon into small pieces and place in the pot. Brown the bacon. Remove, but save drippings.
- Add butter, onion, garlic, parsley, bay leaves, and fish. Saute for 5 minutes. Add thyme and salt and pepper.
- Add half and half. Bring to a boil.
- Serve immediately in soup bowls with Sherry
- Serve with crusty bread and salad.

# FISH CHOWDER

Serves 8

4 large potatoes, peeled and diced
½ pound bacon
½ stick butter
1 medium onion
2 cloves garlic, minced
2 stalks celery, chopped

2 pounds rockfish fillet
2 quarts half and half
1 Tbls. Worcestershire sauce
Salt and pepper to taste
Dash of Tabasco
16 littleneck clams
1 pound cooked shrimp, peeled and deveined

- In a large pot boil the potatoes until just tender. Remove.
- Cut the bacon into small pieces and place in the pot. Brown the bacon. Remove, but save drippings.
- Add butter, onion, garlic, celery and fish. Saute for 5 minutes.
- Add other ingredients. Bring to a boil.
- Serve immediately in soup bowls with crusty bread and salad.

# COLD CUCUMBER SOUP

Serves 8

½ stick butter
4 green onions, sliced
4 large red bliss potatoes, peeled and sliced
6 cups chicken stock
¼ cup dill

1½ cups milk
2 cups sour cream
2 large cucumbers, peeled and diced
½ cup chives, snipped

- ◆ Melt butter in large pot and add onions and potatoes. Cook until potatoes are just tender, about 15 minutes.
- ◆ Cool and puree in food processor. Place in large bowl. Add rest of ingredients. Cover and store overnight.
- ◆ Serve in bowls with chives and a dollop of sour cream.

# CURRIED ZUCCHINI SOUP

Serves 6

½ stick butter
2 medium zucchini, sliced
1 large onion, chopped
3 cloves garlic, minced

1 Tbsl. curry
½ teaspoon ginger
4 cups chicken broth
2 cups heavy cream

- ◆ In a large pot melt the butter. Add the zucchini and onion. Saute until tender. Add garlic.
- ◆ Place in food processor and add curry and ginger.
- ◆ Return to pan and add rest of ingredients.
- ◆ Serve warm or chilled with sour cream and herbs – parsley, chives, and green onion, chopped.

# TOMATO SOUP

Serves 8

½ stick butter
3 cloves garlic, minced
2 stalks celery, chopped
1 medium onion, chopped
1 carrot, peeled and sliced
1 small zucchini, peeled and chopped
6 large tomatoes, chopped

¼ cup brown sugar
1 teaspoon marjoram
¼ cup fresh basil, chopped
2 bay leaves
1 teaspoon curry powder
1 teaspoon fresh ground pepper
4 cups chicken broth
2 cups half and half

- ♦ Melt butter in a large pot. Add garlic, celery, onion, carrots, zucchini and tomatoes. Saute until just tender. Add brown sugar, marjoram, basil, bay leaves, curry, pepper and chicken broth. Add half and half.
- ♦ Serve hot or chilled garnished with fresh basil leaves and a dollop of sour cream.

# TOMATO SOUP

Serves 6

2 Tbls. butter
4 green onions, chopped
2 carrots, chopped
¼ cup fresh basil, chopped

4 cups V8 juice
2 cups consommé
Sour cream
Chives

- ♦ In a sauce pan melt the butter and sauté the onions and carrots.
- ♦ Add basil and V8 juice. Just before serving stir in consommé.
- ♦ Serve in bowls garnished with sour cream and chives.

# TOMATO SOUP

Serves 4

½ stick butter
4 large tomatoes, chopped
2 green onions, chopped
2 cloves garlic, minced
2 bay leaves

1 Tbls. sugar
1 teaspoon pepper
2 cups heavy cream
¼ cup fresh basil, chopped

- ◆ Melt the butter in a pot. Stir in tomatoes, onions, garlic, bay leaves, sugar and pepper. Bring to a boil. Simmer until tomatoes are tender, about 10 minutes.
- ◆ Stir in cream. Heat but do not boil.
- ◆ Serve hot or chilled garnished with fresh basil.
- ◆ Oregano can be substituted for the basil

# PUMPKIN CHOWDER

Serves 6-8

½ stick butter
1 medium onion, chopped
4 cups fresh corn
2 cups chicken broth
2 cups canned pumpkin
4 cups half and half

½ teaspoon salt
1 teaspoon pepper
2 Tbls. fresh grated ginger
½ teaspoon nutmeg
¼ teaspoon cloves
Parsley

- ◆ Melt the butter and add onion and corn. Cook for 5 minutes. Add rest of ingredients, except parsley. Bring to a boil. Simmer for 10 minutes.
- ◆ Serve in bowls garnished with parsley.

# BROCCOLI SOUP

Serves 6

1 large bunch broccoli
½ stick butter
½ cup flour
5 cups chicken stock

1 cup heavy cream
½ teaspoon nutmeg
Salt, pepper
Chives

- ◆ Blanche broccoli in a large pot. Remove broccoli and cut in small pieces.
- ◆ Melt butter in pot. Stir in flour. Add chicken stock until it just begins to thicken.
- ◆ Put in food processor until just blended.
- ◆ Return to pot. Stir in cream and nutmeg.
- ◆ Serve hot or chilled in bowls. Garnish with snipped chives.

# ONION SOUP

Serves 8

5 cups onions, thinly sliced
½ stick butter
1 tablespoon olive oil
1 teaspoon salt
¼ teaspoon sugar
3 tablespoons flour

2 quarts boiling beef broth
½ cup dry Sherry
Salt and pepper
Challah bread, sliced and toasted
½ pound Gruyere cheese, slivered

- ◆ Cook onions in butter and olive oil in covered pan for 15 minutes, stirring occasionally. Uncover, raise heat and stir.
- ◆ Add salt and sugar. Cook 30-40 minutes until onions are a deep golden brown. Stir in flour.
- ◆ Add beef broth, wine, salt and pepper. Simmer partially covered for 30-40 minutes.
- ◆ Pour into a soup tureen or individual soup bowls. Top with toasted bread and cheese.
- ◆ This can also be put in a baking dish and put under the boiler until the cheese just bubbles.

# AVOCADO SOUP

Serves 4

2 large ripe avocadoes, peeled, stones and diced
1 Tbls. lemon juice
1 teaspoon curry powder
½ teaspoon kosher salt
½ teaspoon fresh ground pepper
Lemon slices

2 cups chicken stock
2 cups cream
½ teaspoon cayenne
Parsley
Sour Cream
Lemon slices

- ◆ Combine the avocado, lemon juice, curry, salt and pepper in a food processor.
- ◆ In a sauce pan heat the stock to a boil. Add avocado mixture, cream and cayenne.
- ◆ Serve warm or chilled with parsley, a dollop of sour cream and lemon slice.

# WATERCRESS AND ASPARAGUS SOUP

Serves 6

½ stick butter
1 large leek, chopped
2 bunches watercress, stems removed

½ pound asparagus, chopped
4 cups chicken broth
2 cups heavy cream
1 teaspoon fresh ground pepper
Toasted sliced almonds

- ◆ In a large sauce pan melt ½ the butter. Sautee the leeks until just tender about 7 minutes. Stir in the watercress and add the stock.
- ◆ Place in a food processor and puree.
- ◆ Melt the rest of the butter and sauté asparagus for 3 minutes.
- ◆ Add the asparagus, cream and pepper to the puree.
- ◆ Pour into soup bowls and garnish with the almonds.

# CARROT SOUP

Serves 4-6

½ stick butter
1 large leek, sliced
4 cloves garlic, minced
1 pound carrots, sliced
2 large tomatoes

4 cups chicken stock
1 cup heavy cream
½ cup basil, chopped
Salt and pepper, to taste

- In a large sauce pan melt the butter. Saute leeks and carrots until tender.
- Add tomatoes and stock. Simmer for 20 minutes. Cool.
- Pour into food processor and blend until smooth.
- Return to pan and add cream, salt and pepper to taste.
- Serve warm or chilled, garnished with basil.

# PEANUT SOUP

Serves 8

1 stick butter
1 small onion, chopped
1 celery stalk, chopped finely
¼ cup flour

8 cups chicken stock
2 cups peanut butter
1 cup salted peanuts

- Melt butter and add onion and celery. Stir in flour and stock. Add peanut butter. Cook until smooth.
- Serve in bowls and garnish with peanuts.

# SPLIT PEA SOUP

Serves 6

1 pound green split peas
1 Virginia ham bone with some
meat
1 large onion, chopped

1 teaspoon marjoram
2 celery stalks, chopped
2 carrots, peeled and sliced
2 quarts water

- Place all ingredients in a large pot. Bring to a boil. Reduce heat and simmer 1 ½ -2 hours.
- Serve in bowls.

# SPINACH SOUP

Serves 4

½ stick butter
½ pound baby spinach
1 medium leek, chopped
¼ cup flour

1½ cups chicken stock
2 cups cream
½ teaspoon nutmeg
Salt and pepper

- Melt the butter in a sauce pan. Stir in the leek and spinach. Add flour and stock until thickened.
- Add rest of ingredients.
- Serve hot in bowls and garnished with fresh basil or parsley.
- For a finer soup put cooked spinach and leek through food processor until smooth.

# BROCCOLI STILTON SOUP

Serves 6

½ stick butter
3 green onions, chopped
3 celery stalks, chopped
1 pound broccoli heads, chopped
2 carrots, sliced

4 cups chicken broth
½ pound Stilton cheese
2 cups cream
¼ cup Sherry
Salt and pepper to taste

- Melt the butter in a pot. Add onions, celery, broccoli, and carrots. Stir in chicken broth.
- Put in food processor until pureed. Place back in pot. Heat.
- Add cheese and cream, stirring until thickened. Add Sherry and salt and pepper to taste.
- Serve in bowls.

# TURNIP SOUP

Serves 8

2 medium onions, sliced
1 stick butter
6 turnips, peeled and diced
¼ cup flour
8 cups chicken broth

2 egg yolks, beaten
1 cup heavy cream
Salt and pepper to taste
¼ cup fresh parsley

- Melt ½ stick butter in a sauce pan. Add onions and turnips and cook 20 minutes, or until tender.
- Add rest of butter and stir in flour. Add stock and stir until slightly thickened.
- Place in food processor and puree. Pour back into the pan and add the egg yolks.
- Stir in cream and salt and pepper.
- Serve in bowls garnished with parsley.

# CHICKEN STEW

Serves 6

½ stick butter
4 large boneless chicken breasts
4 cups water
4 cloves garlic, minced
½ cup red bell pepper, chopped
½ cup yellow pepper, chopped
4 green onions, chopped

1 large ripe tomato, chopped
2 cans black beans
Juice of 1 lime
1 teaspoon cumin
1 teaspoon oregano
Dash of hot pepper sauce
¼ cup dark rum

- ◆ Melt the butter in a large pot. Brown chicken on both sides - about 10 minutes. Remove breasts and cut into small pieces.
- ◆ Add all ingredients, except rum to the pot.
- ◆ Bring to a boil. Simmer for 1 hour. Add rum.
- ◆ Serve over rice and top with chopped green onions

# CURRIED CHICKEN SOUP

Serves 4

½ stick butter
Salt and pepper
2 large boneless chicken breasts
1 small onion, chopped
1 stalk celery, chopped
2 carrots, sliced
1 cup fresh corn

2 red bliss potatoes, diced
2 cups water
2 Tbls. cilantro, chopped
2 Tbls. fresh parsley, chopped
2 Tbls fresh ginger, grated
1 Tbls curry
2 cups heavy cream

- ◆ Melt the butter in a pot. Rub the chicken with a small amount of salt and pepper. Brown the chicken for about 10 minutes. Remove from pot and cut into small pieces.
- ◆ Add the onion, celery, carrots, corn, potatoes and water in the pot. Bring to a boil. Simmer until vegetables are just tender.
- ◆ Add chicken, cilantro, parsley, ginger and curry. Add more for taste.
- ◆ Stir in cream.
- ◆ Serve hot or chilled garnished with cilantro.

# SEAFOOD

Chesapeake Bay Crab Cakes

*"He was a bold man that first eat an oyster"*
Jonathan Swift in <u>Polite Conversation</u>

*"Fish lying so thicke with their heads above the water, as for want of our nets (our barge driving amongst them) we attempted to catch them with a frying pan, but we found it a bad instrument to catch fish with."*
Captain John Smith of Jamestown

The Chesapeake Bay has been home to oystering since the early 19th c. Chesapeake Bay skipjacks are the last commercial sailing vessels in the United States. The dredge boats once numbered in the thousands. Today only about a dozen remain. Skipjacks are limited to one hundred and fifty bushels of oysters a day. On Monday and Tuesday the boats may use a yawl boat with an engine to push the boat. Other days they may only use their sails. The dredging season starts November 1st and ends March 31st. The skipjacks can only dredge in a limited number of oyster bars and tributaries of the Bay. They have a crew of six on board.

In 1854 when a Coast and Geodetic survey of the Chesapeake Bay found large number of oyster beds in Tangier Sound, Crisfield found itself on the map. In1868 the Eastern Shore Railway built a terminal in Crisfield. Seafood could now be transported more quickly and refrigerated. Crisfield was then called the "Seafood Capital of the World". Albert LaVallette settled on Hammock Point and cultivated terrapin by using waste from crab pickings. He eventually went to Philadelphia and other cities touting his "LaVallette Diamondback Terrapin", his own recipe for terrapin stew. By signing contracts with only the most exclusive restaurants, he made a killing on selling terrapin. Soon the Bay was depleted of almost all terrapin and the Maryland legislature passed laws to protect them. In the meantime Mr. LaVallette had made his fortune and built a large home in Crisfield. Isaac Solomon who had patented a pasteurizing canning process, brought his ideas to Crisfield and set up a processing plant here. By 1910 the Crisfield Customs House had the largest registry of sailing vessels in the U.S. Sadly most of the canning and processing facilities are closed down.

Before the opening of the Bay Bridge a ferry ran from Matapeake. Kent Narrows was noted for seafood processing, but now has only three remaining establishments. The W.H. Harris Company was founded by William Holton Harris in 1947. The Holton Harris packing house was replaced by the Crab House Restaurant in 1991.

Tilghman Island is one of the main places for oystering on the Chesapeake. In 1897 the Harrison family opened the Tilghman Packing plant, but it was closed in 1977. Tilghman Island is home to some of the last skipjacks (oyster boats) on the Chesapeake. The *H.M. Krentz*, owned by Ed Farley and the *Rebecca T. Ruark*, owned by Capt. Wade H. Murphy, Jr. still dredge oysters, and during the off-oyster season take passengers for trips around the Bay.

Wachapreague, on the Eastern Shore of Virginia, is called the "Flounder Capital of the World".

# FRIED SOFT-SHELL CRABS

Serves 4

| | |
|---|---|
| 12 soft-shelled crabs | 1 teaspoon Old Bay or Wye |
| 1 cup panko | River seasoning |
| | Oil |

- ◆ Combine the panko and seasoning in a bowl. Dredge the crabs in the mixture.
- ◆ Heat the oil in a skillet. Fry the crabs until browned on both sides.
- ◆ Serve with Remoulade Sauce or tartar sauce and lemon slices.
- ◆ Flour can be substituted for the panko.

# SAUTEED SOFT SHELL CRABS

Soft-shell crabs come into season the end of April when the crabs lose their hard shell. They are my favorite spring dish served with fresh asparagus and new potatoes.

Serves 4

12 soft-shell crabs
1 cup panko
½ stick butter

½ cup toasted almonds
4 lemon slices

- ◆ Put the panko in a bowl and gently coat crabs.
- ◆ Melt the butter in a skillet. Saute crabs on both sides for about 3 minutes each, until just browned. Remove and sprinkle with almonds.
- ◆ Serve with lemon slices.


# SOFT-SHELL CRABS ALMONDINE

Serves 4

4 cloves garlic, minced
1 cup flour
12 soft-shell crabs
½ stick butter

½ cup fresh parsley, chopped
½ cup slivered toasted almonds
Lemon slices

- ◆ In a bowl combine the garlic and flour. Dredge the crabs in the mixture.
- ◆ Melt the butter in a skillet. Saute crabs on both sides.
- ◆ Serve with parsley, almonds and lemon slices.

# SOFT-SHELL CRABS WITH WATERCRESS SAUCE

Serves 4

1 cup flour                                 ½ stick butter
12 soft-shell crabs

- ◆ Put the flour in a bowl and dredge crabs.
- ◆ Melt butter in a skillet. Brown crabs on both sides.
- ◆ Serve with watercress sauce.

*Watercress Sauce*

1 bunch watercress, chopped,     ½ teaspoon paprika
stems removed                          ¼ teaspoon cayenne
1 cup mayonnaise                     Juice of ½ lemon
2 cloves garlic, minced

- ◆ Combine the ingredients in a bowl.

# CRAB CAKES

4 crab cakes

1 pound crab meat                    2 tablespoons mayonnaise
2 Tbls. bread crumbs               Dash of Old Bay or Wye River
1 egg                                         Seasoning
1 tsp. Worcestershire sauce     Butter
1 teaspoon Dijon mustard

- ◆ With a fork carefully combine the ingredients in a bowl.
- ◆ Shape into cakes. Saute in butter until brown on each side.
- ◆ Serve on sourdough rolls with tartar sauce and lemon

# CRAB CAKES

We like our crab cakes just plain, no veggies or anything else added. However, these are good too.

4 crab cakes

1 pound crab meat
2 Tbls. bread crumbs
1 egg
1 tsp. Worcestershire sauce
1 teaspoon Dijon mustard
2 tablespoons mayonnaise

Dash of Old Bay or Wye River
Seasoning
2 green onions, chopped
¼ cup red bell pepper, chopped
¼ cup celery, chopped
2 Tbls. parsley
Butter

♦ With a fork carefully combine the ingredients in a bowl.
♦ Shape into cakes. Saute in butter until brown on each side.
Serve on sourdough rolls with tartar sauce and lemon

# DEVILED CRAB

Serves 4

1 stick butter
1 green onion, chopped
¼ cup flour
1½ cups half and half
Juice of ½ lemon
1 teaspoon dry mustard
½ teaspoon Worcestershire sauce

¼ teaspoon cayenne
2 Tbls. parsley
1 pound fresh crab meat
½ cup bread crumbs
4 lemon slices
½ teaspoon paprika

♦ Preheat oven to 425°
♦ Melt ½ stick butter in a sauce pan and add green onion and flour. Stir in half and half. Add lemon juice, mustard, Worcestershire, cayenne and parsley. Remove from heat.
♦ Fold in crab. Spoon into 4 large scallop shells.
♦ Sprinkle with bread crumbs and dot with remaining butter.
♦ Bake for 15 minutes or until bubbly.
♦ Serve immediately with lemon slices and paprika.

# CRAB GUMBO

Serves 6-8

2 pounds crab meat
½ stick butter
½ cup flour
3 scallions, sliced
½ red bell pepper, chopped
1 pound Andouille sausage
1 stalk celery, chopped
4 cloves garlic, minced

4 large tomatoes, chopped
½ pound okra, trimmed
4 bay leaves
1 teaspoon thyme
2 Tbls. fresh basil
½ teaspoon cayenne
Dash of Tabasco
3 cups chicken stock

- In a large pot melt the butter and add the flour, stirring until the mixtures thickens and turns brown. Do not burn.
- Stir in the scallions, celery garlic tomatoes, okra, and bay leaves. Heat until the vegetables are just tender. Add thyme, basil, cayenne and Tabasco. Stir in stock.
- Brown the sausage in a skillet. Add the sausage to vegetables.
- Bring to a boil and simmer for ½ hour or longer. Add crab.
- Serve over cooked rice.
- Shrimp can be added, or use instead of crab.

# CRAB AU GRATIN

Serves 4

½ stick butter
¼ cup flour
1½ cups half and half
2 green onion, chopped
½ red bell pepper, chopped

¼ cup red pimentos
1 pound crab meat
½ cup fine bread crumbs
½ cup Parmesan cheese, freshly grated

- Preheat oven to 350°
- Melt the butter in a sauce pan. Stir in flour and half and half until thickened. Stir in onion, pepper, pimentos and crab.
- Pour into greased baking dish. Top with bread crumbs and cheese. Bake 15-20 minutes until bubbling and slightly browned.
- Serve with rice.

# STEAMED CRABS

Serves 6-8

2 dozen crabs
2 cans beer
2 cups vinegar

½ cup Old Bay or Wye River
Seasoning

- Place the crabs in a large pot with the beer, vinegar and Old Bay Seasoning. Steam 20-30 minutes, or until crabs are red.
- Serve crabs hot outside on a table covered with newspapers or brown paper.
- Have plenty of paper napkins, mallets, and crab picks available.
- To pick a crab, flip the crab over, open the apron and then the top shell.
- Discard the gills and devil.
- Break the crab in half. Pull the legs and claws off.
- Suck the meat out of the legs and save the claws.
- With a paring knife split each half of the crab and take the meat out. Break the claws in half with a mallet.

# BAKED CRAB AND HAM

Serves 4

½ stick butter
¼ cup flour
1 ½ cups half and half
1 Tbls. Dijon mustard
Juice of 1 lemon
¼ teaspoon cayenne
½ red bell pepper, chopped

1 stalk celery, chopped
2 green onions, chopped
¼ pound thinly sliced Smithfield ham
1 pound crab meat
½ cup bread crumbs
½ cup parmesan cheese

- Preheat oven to 350°
- Melt the butter in a sauce pan. Stir in flour and half and half. Add mustard, lemon juice, and cayenne. Add vegetables. Stir in crab.
- Line a greased baking dish with the ham. Pour the crab mixture on top. Bake 15-20 minutes until bubbling and browned.
- Serve with rice.

# CRAB AND CHICKEN IN PUFF PASTRY

Serves 4

2 Tbls butter
2 large boneless chicken breasts
¼ cup parmesan cheese
2 Tbls. butter
¼ pound baby spinach
2 cloves garlic, minced

1 pound lump crab meat
2 Tbls. heavy cream
2 Tbls. lemon juice
Puff pastry
1 egg, beaten

- Preheat oven to 425°
- Place the chicken in a baking dish and top with butter and parmesan cheese. Bake for ½ hour. Remove from oven and dice.
- In a skillet melt the butter and sauté spinach and garlic until just limp.
- In a bowl combine the spinach, chicken and crab with cream and lemon juice. Divide mixture into fourths.
- Roll the pastry into 4 squares about ¼" thick.
- Place the crab/chicken mixture on the pastry. Dampen the edges of the pastry, fold over mixture and press to seal edges with a little water.
- Place on a baking sheet and brush with the egg.
- Bake in the oven for 25 minutes or until pastry is browned.
- Serve with cognac mushroom cream sauce.

*Cognac Mushroom Cream Sauce*

1 stick butter
½ pound mushrooms, sliced
¼ cup flour

1 cup half and half
½ cup heavy cream
¼ cup Cognac

- In a sauce pan melt the butter. Stir in mushrooms for 2 minutes. Add flour. Stir in half and half and cream. Then add Cognac.

# CRAB CROQUETTES

Makes 4 Croquettes

2 Tbls. butter
2 Tbls. flour
½ cup half and half
1 egg, beaten
1 teaspoon Worcestershire sauce

Dash of Tabasco
1 pound fresh crab meat
1 cup Italian bread crumbs
Vegetable oil
Tartar Sauce

- ♦ In a sauce pan melt the butter and stir in flour. Pour the half and half in slowly until thickened. Remove from heat.
- ♦ Stir in egg. Add Worcestershire and Tabasco sauces. Fold in crab meat.
- ♦ Divide mixture into 4 portions. Shape into croquette or ball. Roll in bread crumbs.
- ♦ Pour vegetable oil into skillet. Fry the croquettes until browned on all sides.
- ♦ Arrange on platter. Serve at once with tartar sauce or remoulade.

# BAKED CRAB

Serves 4

½ stick butter, melted
1 pound crab meat
1 cup fine bread crumbs
½ red bell pepper, chopped
2 green onions, chopped

2 cloves garlic, minced
¼ cup dry white wine
2 Tbls. lime juice
¼ cup parsley, chopped
Dash of cayenne

- ♦ Preheat oven to 350°
- ♦ Combine all the ingredients in a bowl.
- ♦ Pour into greased baking dish.
- ♦ Bake 20 minutes or until just browned.
- ♦ Small shrimp can be substituted for the crab.
- ♦ Serve with rice.

# CRAB REMOULADE

Serves 4

2 large ripe avocados, cut in half
and pitted
Red leaf lettuce
1 pound crab meat

Cherry tomatoes
Cucumber sliced
8 deviled eggs
Paprika

- ◆ Place the avocado halves on top of lettuce leaves on 4 plates.
- ◆ Combine the crab and remoulade. Spoon into the avocado.
- ◆ Sprinkle with small amount of paprika.
- ◆ Place the cherry tomatoes, cucumbers and eggs around avocado.

*Remoulade*

1 cup mayonnaise
2 Tbls. Dijon mustard
2 Tbls. tarragon vinegar
1 Tbls. tarragon
2 Tbls. parsley, chopped
2 cloves garlic, minced

½ stalk celery, chopped finely
Dash of Tabasco
1 green onions, chopped
1 Tbls. capers
½ teaspoon chervil
1 Tbls lemon juice

Combine all ingredients in a bowl.

# SEAFOOD CURRY

Serves 4

½ stick butter
2 green onions, chopped
½ pound mushrooms, sliced
½ red bell pepper, chopped
¼ cup flour
1½ cups chicken stock
1 Tbls. curry

1 Tbls. fresh grated ginger
½ teaspoon cumin
½ teaspoon chili powder
½ pound medium shrimp
½ pound lobster meat
½ pound crab meat

- ◆ Melt the butter in a skillet. Add onions, mushrooms, and pepper.
  Stir in flour and add stock and spices. Stir in seafood.
- ◆ Serve hot over rice with condiments.

# ROCKFISH BOUILLABAISSE

Serves 8

3 pounds rockfish filets
1 small onion, chopped
2 large tomatoes, chopped
2 cloves garlic, minced
¼ cup parsley, chopped
Pinch of saffron

¼ cup olive oil
1 bay leaf
½ teaspoon salt
1 teaspoon fresh ground pepper
Sliced French bread

- ♦ Put all the ingredients, except bread in a covered pot. Just cover with water. Bring to a boil. Simmer for 15 minutes.
- ♦ Serve in a soup bowl over slices of bread.


# BAKED ROCKFISH

Serves 6

1 whole rockfish, approximately 5 to 6 pounds, cleaned and washed
½ stick butter
2 green onions, chopped
1 stalk celery, chopped
½ red pepper, chopped
¼ pound mushrooms, sliced
2 cups bread crumbs

½ cup toasted almonds
¼ cup fresh parsley, chopped
1 teaspoon tarragon
Salt and pepper to taste
½ stick butter, melted

- ♦ Preheat oven to 350°
- ♦ Melt the butter in a skillet. Add onions, celery, pepper and mushrooms. Cook for 3 minutes. Add other ingredients, except melted butter.
- ♦ Line a large baking dish with foil. Place the fish on foil. Sprinkle with a little salt and pepper.
- ♦ Stuff the cavity of the fish with the crumb mixture. Pour the melted butter over the fish.
- ♦ Bake for 1 hour or until fish flakes easily with a fork.
- ♦ Serve on a fish platter garnished with lemon slices, toasted almonds and parsley.

# BAKED ROCKFISH

Serves 6

2 ½ pounds rockfish fillet
¼ cup soy sauce
¼ cup lime juice
2 Tbls. olive oil
2 Tbls. tomato paste
12 cherry tomatoes, sliced

3 cloves garlic, minced
1 Tbls. fresh oregano
½ red bell pepper, chopped
1 teaspoon pepper
2 green onions, chopped

- ♦ Preheat oven to 350°
- ♦ In a bowl combine all the ingredients except rockfish.
- ♦ Place the rockfish in a baking dish. Cover with soy mixture.
- ♦ Put in oven and bake ½ hour.
- ♦ Serve with rice.

# BAKED ROCKFISH

Serves 6

2 ½ pounds rockfish filet
½ cup green pepper
½ cup red pepper
1 large tomato, chopped
2 green onions, chopped
½ pound mushrooms, sliced
1 Tbls. fresh oregano

¼ cup fresh parsley, chopped
1 cup pitted Greek olives
3 cloves garlic, minced
Juice of 1 lemon
¼ cup olive oil
6 lemon wedges

- ♦ Place the fish in a baking dish. Top with the other ingredients. Bake ½ hour.
- ♦ Serve on fish platter.

# BAKED ROCKFISH

Serves 6

½ stick butter, melted
½ cup capers
2 teaspoons kosher salt
¼ cup olive oil

1 teaspoon fresh ground black pepper
¼ cup lemon juice
¼ cup parsley, chopped
2 ½ pounds rockfish fillet

- ♦ Preheat oven to 350°
- ♦ Place rockfish in baking dish. Cover with other ingredients.
- ♦ Bake 30 minutes.
- ♦ Serve on fish platter with lemon slices.

# BAKED ROCKFISH WITH CRAB

Serves 6

2 ½ pounds rockfish fillets
½ stick butter
¼ cup flour
1 cup half and half
1 cup dry white wine

2 Tbls. fresh parsley, chopped
1 teaspoon fresh thyme
½ pound baby spinach leaves
1 pound crab meat
1 lemon

- ♦ Preheat oven to 450°
- ♦ In a sauce pan melt the butter. Stir in the flour then half and half. Stir in wine, parsley, thyme, and spinach.
- ♦ Place the rockfish in a greased baking dish. Divide the crab meat between the fillets. Top with spinach mixture. Sprinkle with lemon juice.
- ♦ Bake 15 minutes or until just browned.
- ♦ Serve with rice.

# BAKED ROCKFISH

Serves 6

2 ½ pounds rockfish fillet
¼ cup capers
2 large tomatoes, chopped
3 cloves garlic, minced
1 small leek, chopped

3 chives, snipped
¼ cup lemon juice
3 Tbls. butter
3 Tbls. olive oil

- ◆ Preheat oven to 350°
- ◆ Lay the rockfish in a baking dish. Top with other ingredients.
- ◆ Bake for ½ hour.
- ◆ Place on fish platter and garnish with parsley.

# BAKED ROCKFISH

Serves 6

6 pound rockfish, cleaned
Sea salt and fresh ground pepper
4 shallots, chopped
4 slices bacon
½ pound baby spinach
4 thick slices French bread, cubed
1 cup cream
2 eggs

¼ cup almonds
2 Tbls. basil, chopped
½ teaspoon sage
2 Tbls. parsley, chopped
2 Tbls. chives, snipped
1 cup dry white wine
Juice of 1 lemon
Lemon slices
Fresh parsley

- ◆ Preheat oven to 350°
- ◆ Rub the inside of the fish with some salt and pepper. Place in a greased baking dish.
- ◆ In a skillet cook the bacon with the shallots. Stir in the spinach.
- ◆ In a bowl combine the cream and eggs. Soak the bread in the mixture. Stir into spinach mixture.
- ◆ Add nuts and herbs.
- ◆ Stuff the fish with the mixture. Pour the wine and lemon juice over the fish.
- ◆ Bake for 60 minutes, or until fish is just browned.
- ◆ Serve on a platter with fish juices and garnished with lemon slices and parsley.

# BAKED ROCKFISH

Serves 6

¼ cup lemon juice
2 Tbls. olive oil
2 tomatoes, chopped
1 15 oz. can artichoke hearts

1 cup fresh corn
2 green onions, chopped
¼ cup cilantro, chopped
2 ½ pounds rockfish fillet

- Preheat oven to 350°
- Place the rockfish in a baking dish. Top with ingredients.
- Bake 25-30 minutes, until tender.
- Serve with lemon slices.

# ROCKFISH WITH LEMON SAUCE

Serves 4

1 ½ pounds rockfish fillets
Juice of 1 lemon

Juice of 1 lime

- Marinate in lemon and lime juice. Grill.
- Serve with lemon sauce and sliced lemons

*Lemon Sauce*

1 stick butter, softened
½ teaspoon kosher salt
Dash cayenne

Zest of 1 lemon
Juice of 1 lemon
2 egg yolks, beaten

- Melt butter in a sauce pan. Add salt, cayenne, zest and lemon juice. Slowly stir in egg yolks, beating until sauce is thickened and a light yellow.

73

# GRILLED ROCKFISH

Serves 6

¼ cup olive oil
¼ cup lemon juice
¼ cup Chardonnay
2 Tbls. Dijon mustard

1 Tbls. Chili powder
¼ cup cilantro
2 ½ pounds rockfish fillet

- ◆ Combine all ingredients in a bowl. Marinate for at least two hours in refrigerator
- ◆ Grill on a BBQ until just browned on each side.
- ◆ Serve with lemon slices and rest of marinade.

# ROCKFISH WITH GARLIC BASIL SAUCE

Serves 6

2 ½ pounds rockfish fillet
Juice of 1 lemon

¼ cup olive oil

- ◆ Rub fish with lemon juice and olive oil.
- ◆ Grill on BBQ until just browned on each side.
- ◆ Serve with garlic basil sauce.

*Garlic/Basil Sauce*

2 bunches basil
4 cloves garlic

¼ cup olive oil

- ◆ Combine all ingredients in a food processor.

# ROCKFISH WITH TOMATO CREAM SAUCE

Serves 6

2 ½ pounds rockfish fillet
½ stick butter
¼ cup flour
1 cup cream
½ cup white wine

2 large tomatoes, chopped
¼ cup fresh basil chopped
2 green onions, chopped
3 cloves garlic, minced
¼ cup parmesan cheese

- Preheat oven to 350°
- Melt the butter in a sauce pan. Stir in flour and cream. Add wine and other ingredients.
- Place the fish in a greased baking dish.
- Top with sauce.
- Bake ½ hour, or until just browned and bubbling.
- Serve with rice.

# FRIED ROCKFISH

Serves 6

2½ pounds rockfish fillet
½ cup flour
½ panko

½ teaspoon salt
½ teaspoon pepper
Vegetable oil

- In a brown bag shake the rockfish with the other ingredients, except oil.
- In a skillet heat the oil. Brown fish on both sides.
- Serve with lemon caper butter sauce.

*Lemon Caper Butter Sauce*

1 stick butter, softened
¼ cup capers

¼ cup lemon juice

- Combine all ingredients in a bowl

# STUFFED ROCKFISH

Serves 6

5½ pound whole rockfish,
cleaned and washed
2 green onions, chopped
2 stalks celery, chopped
1 large tomato, chopped
2 cups bread crumbs

1 teaspoon thyme
3 slices cooked bacon, crumbled
¼ cup parsley, chopped
½ cup white wine.
½ stick butter, melted

- ◆ Preheat oven to 350°
- ◆ In a bowl combine onions, celery, tomato, breadcrumbs, thyme, bacon, parsley and white wine.
- ◆ Place the rockfish in a large baking dish. Stuff the cavity with the bread mixture.
- ◆ Pour butter over fish.
- ◆ Bake 1 hour.

# STUFFED ROCKFISH

Serves 6

5 ½ pound whole rockfish
2 Tbls. kosher salt
1 teaspoon pepper
½ stick butter
½ pound mushrooms, sliced
3 cloves garlic, minced

½ red bell pepper, chopped
½ cup white wine
¼ cup fresh parsley, chopped
¼ cup lemon juice
2 cups breadcrumbs

- ◆ Preheat oven to 350
- ◆ Rub the outside of the fish with the salt.
- ◆ In a bowl combine the ingredients.
- ◆ Place the fish in a greased baking dish. Stuff with bread mixture.
- ◆ Pour a little olive oil over fish.
- ◆ Bake 1 hour.
- ◆ Serve with lemon slices.

# ROLLED FILETS WITH CRAB

Serves 4

½ stick butter
¼ cup flour
1 cup half and half
½ cup cream
2 chives, snipped
1 tomato, chopped

2 cloves garlic, minced
¼ cup white wine
4 rockfish filets
1 pound crab meat
¼ cup parmesan cheese
¼ cup fine bread crumbs

- ◆ Preheat oven to 350°
- ◆ Melt the butter in a sauce pan. Add flour and stir in half and half and cream until thickened. Stir in chives, tomato, garlic and white wine.
- ◆ In a bowl combine ½ white sauce mixture with crab meat.
- ◆ Divide crab mixture into four parts and spread on rockfish. Roll up fish and secure with a toothpick.
- ◆ Place in greased baking dish. Pour rest of sauce over fillets. Top with parmesan cheese and breadcrumbs. Bake ½ hour.

# ROCKFISH WITH CRAB

Serves 6

6 rockfish fillet
1 pound crab meat

½ pound thin sliced Smithfield ham

- ◆ Preheat oven to 350°
- ◆ Place the rockfish in a greased baking dish.
- ◆ Top each piece with a slice of ham and crab. Top with Bearnaise sauce – p. 202
- ◆ Bake 20-25 minutes, until just bubbling.

# GRILLED ROCKFISH

Serves 6

2 ½ pounds rockfish fillet          ¼ cup lemon juice
2 Tbls. olive oil

- ♦ Rub olive oil and lemon juice on rockfish. Grill on BBQ until just browned. Place on fish platter.

3 scallions, chopped                ¼ cup olive oil
1 cup pitted black and green        ¼ cup white wine
olives                              12 cherry tomatoes
1 red bell pepper, chopped          2 Tbls. balsamic vinegar

- ♦ Combine ingredients in a bowl. Serve over rockfish.


# ROCKFISH AND CRAB BAKE

Serves 8

2 pounds rockfish filets            ½ pound mushrooms
2 pounds crab meat shrimp           Chive cream sauce

- ♦ Preheat oven to 350°
- ♦ Place the rockfish in a buttered baking dish. Top with crab, mushrooms and chive cream sauce.
- ♦ Bake ½ hour or until bubbling and just browned.

*Chive Cream Sauce*

1 stick butter                      4 chives, snipped
½ cup flour                         ½ cup dry white wine
2 cups half and half

- ♦ Melt the butter in a sauce pan. Add flour and stir in half and half until thickened. Add chives and wine.

# FRIED OYSTERS

Serves 4-6

1 cup flour
1 cup cornmeal
½ teaspoon kosher salt
1 teaspoon Old Bay or Wye River Seasoning

2 eggs
3 dozen oysters, shucked
Oil

- ♦ In a bowl combine flour, cornmeal, salt and seasoning.
- ♦ Beat the eggs in a second bowl.
- ♦ Dip the oysters in flour mixture, then egg mixture, then flour mixture again.
- ♦ Fry in hot oil in a skillet. Drain on paper towels. Keep warm in the oven.
- ♦ Serve with tartar or horseradish sauce.


# FRIED OYSTERS

Serves 4-6

3 dozen shucked oysters
1 cup flour
1 cup panko

1 teaspoon Old Bay or Wye Island Seasoning
2 eggs

- ♦ In a bowl combine flour, panko, salt and seasoning.
- ♦ Beat the eggs in a second bowl.
- ♦ Dip the oysters in panko mixture, then egg mixture, then
- ♦ panko mixture again.
- ♦ Fry in hot oil in a skillet. Drain on paper towels. Keep warm in the oven.
- ♦ Serve with jalapeno mayonnaise sauce

*Jalapeno Mayonnaise Sauce*

1 cup mayonnaise
3 jalapeno, seeded and chopped

¼ cup cilantro, chopped
2 Tbls. lemon juice

- ♦ Combine the ingredients in a bowl

# BAKED OYSTERS

Serves 4-6

1 teaspoon pepper
¼ teaspoon cayenne
1 teaspoon tarragon
1 teaspoon oregano
2 Tbls. parsley
3 cloves garlic, minced

2 green onions, chopped
½ red bell pepper, chopped
3 dozen oysters, shucked
1 cup bread crumbs
½ stick butter, melted

- ♦ Preheat oven to 350°
- ♦ Combine all ingredients except bread crumbs and butter in greased baking dish.
- ♦ Top with bread crumbs and drizzle with butter.
- ♦ Bake for 20 minutes until just bubbling.


# BAKED OYSTERS

Serves 6

36 shucked oysters with liquor
1 stick butter
½ cup flour
1 ½ cups half and half
½ cup white wine or sherry
½ pound mushrooms, sliced

2 cloves garlic, minced
2 cloves shallot, chopped
½ pound thinly sliced Smithfield ham
½ cup parmesan cheese
½ cup breadcrumbs

- ♦ Preheat oven to 350°
- ♦ Melt the butter in a sauce pan. Add flour and half and half. Stir until thickened. Add wine and ½ cup oyster liquor.
- ♦ Line the baking dish with the Smithfield ham. Top with oysters, mushrooms, garlic and shallot.
- ♦ Sprinkle with parmesan cheese and breadcrumbs.
- ♦ Bake 25 minutes or until bubbling and just browned.

# OYSTERS AU GRATIN

Serves 6

36 shucked oysters with liquor
1 stick butter
½ cup flour
1 ½ cups half and half
½ cup white wine or sherry
½ pound mushrooms, sliced

¼ cup basil, chopped
2 Tbls. parsley
3 cloves garlic, minced
½ cup parmesan cheese
½ cup bread crumbs

- Preheat oven to 350°
- Melt the butter in a sauce pan. Add flour and half and half. Stir until thickened. Add wine and ½ cup oyster liquor.
- In a baking dish combine the oysters, basil parsley and garlic.
- Sprinkle with parmesan cheese and breadcrumbs.
- Bake 25 minutes or until bubbling and just browned.

# OYSTER PIE

Serves 6

3 dozen oysters, shucked
½ red bell pepper, chopped
2 green onion, chopped

1 Tbls. Worcestershire sauce
2 cup Saltine cracker crumbs
1 stick butter, melted

- Preheat oven to 400°
- Combine 1st 4 ingredients. Place ½ mixture in greased glass baking dish. Top with ½ saltines and ½ butter. Repeat.
- Bake for 20 minutes, or just bubbling.

# POACHED OYSTERS

Serves 4

| | |
|---|---|
| 1 quart oysters with liquor | 2 shallots, minced |
| 1 cup white wine | 1 Tbls. oregano |
| 2 cloves garlic, minced | 1 Tbls. basil |

- ♦ In a sauce pan cook the oysters in liquor, wine and herbs.

| | |
|---|---|
| ½ pound mushrooms, sliced | 1 parmesan cheese |
| ¼ pound thin sliced Smithfield ham | |

- ♦ Preheat oven to 350°
- ♦ Place oysters in baking dish. Top with mushrooms, Smithfield ham and parmesan cheese.
- ♦ Bake until just browned and bubbling.


# FRIED OYSTERS WITH BOURSIN

Serves 4

| | |
|---|---|
| 24 fried oysters - p | 1 container Boursin cheese |
| ½ pound baby spinach | |

- ♦ Place the spinach on 4 plates. Top with oysters and then Boursin.
- ♦ The spinach can also be sautéed and placed on plates.

# JAMBALAYA

Serves 4

1 pound shrimp, cooked, peeled
and deveined
¼ cup dark rum
1 pound Andouille sausage
4 slices bacon
1 small onion, chopped
2 scallions, chopped
1 stalk celery
½ cup red pepper, chopped
½ green pepper, chopped

2 medium tomatoes, chopped
2 cloves garlic, minced
2 bay leaves
¼ cup parsley, chopped
¼ teaspoon cayenne
1 teaspoon salt
1 teaspoon pepper
1 cup rice
2 cups water

- ♦ Combine the shrimp and rum in a bowl. Marinate for at least 4 hours.
- ♦ Preheat oven to 400°
- ♦ Place the sausage in a baking dish and bake for 15 minutes, or until just browned. Remove and cut into pieces.
- ♦ Brown the bacon in a pot. Remove bacon and crumble. Sauté the onion, scallions, celery, and peppers until onions are transparent, in the pot using bacon drippings.
- ♦ Add other vegetables, seasonings, rice and water.
- ♦ Bring to a boil. Reduce heat and cook for 25 minutes.
- ♦ Add shrimp, rum and sausage. Just heat until all ingredients are warm.

# MIXED SEAFOOD GRILL

Serves 6-8

1 pound salmon filets, cut in pieces
1 pound rockfish filets, cut in pieces
1 pound scallops
1 pound medium shrimp, cooked, peeled and deveined

1 red bell pepper, cut in cubes
1 yellow pepper, cut in cubes
1 large red onion, cut in cubes
3 tomatoes, cut in cubes
Juice of 2 lemons
Sour Cream Sauce
Lemon slices

♦ Alternate fish and vegetables on skewers. Sprinkle with lemon juice. Cook for about 5 minutes on each side.
♦ Serve with rice and sour cream and lemon slices.

# FISH STEW

Serves 6

2 Tbls. butter
2 Tbls. olive oil
1 medium onion, chopped
2 celery stalks, chopped
1 small red pepper, chopped
1 carrot, peeled and sliced
4 cloves garlic, minced
2 Tbls. flour
4 large tomatoes, chopped

¼ teaspoon cayenne
2 cups fish or chicken stock
2½ pounds rockfish fillets, cut into small pieces
1 teaspoon oregano
¼ cup fresh basil, chopped
2 Tbls. fresh parsley, chopped
3 cups cooked rice

♦ Melt the butter and heat the olive oil. Stir in onion, celery, pepper, and carrot. Cook for 4 minutes.
♦ Add garlic, tomatoes and cayenne.
♦ Add stock, fish, oregano, basil and parsley. Bring to boil.
♦ Simmer 20 minutes.
♦ Serve stew over rice.

# SEAFOOD LASAGNA

Serves 4-6

1 pound wide noodles
8 oz. cream cheese
8 oz. sour cream
4 green onions, chopped
¼ cup fresh basil, chopped
2 Tbls. butter

½ pound mushrooms, sliced
1 pound rockfish filets, cut into pieces
1 pound crab meat
¼ cup lemon juice

- Preheat oven to 350°
- Cook noodles according to directions. Drain.
- In a bowl combine cream cheese, sour cream, green onions and basil.
- Melt the butter in a skillet and sauté mushrooms with rockfish.
- Stir in crab and lemon juice.
- Put the noodles in the bottom of a baking dish. Top with cream cheese mixture. Then crab mixture.
- Bake ½ hour, or until just browned and bubbling.

# BAKED SHAD ROE

Shad run in the spring. The roe are considered a delicacy.

Serves 4

½ stick butter
½ yellow pepper, chopped
1 small onion, chopped
2 Tbls. flour
2 large tomatoes, chopped

¼ cup parsley, chopped
½ teaspoon salt
½ teaspoon pepper
2 pairs of shad roe

- Preheat oven to 400°
- Melt the butter and add pepper and onion. Cook until just tender. Add flour.
- Stir in tomatoes, parsley, salt and pepper. Bring to boil. Simmer 5 minutes.
- Please the shad roe in a buttered baking dish. Pour tomato mixture over roe.
- Bake 15 minutes.

# POULTRY

The author and her oldest friend, Quinton Hallett (both age 9
months) at "Harmony Hills"

Delaware's nickname "The Blue Hen State" is most appropriate for a state that has raised chickens since the first settlers brought them. During the 1920s chickens became a major industry. Today Delaware is the leading producer of broiler chickens in the United States. This all began by accident in 1923 when Cecile Steele of Ocean View ordered fifty chicks, but instead received 500 barred rock chickens. She raised them and then sold them. Since many of the other farmers in the state had diseased chickens this was very helpful in starting the broiler industry. The shed in which Mrs. Steele raised the chickens is now on display at Delaware Agricultural Museum.

# CHICKEN BREASTS STUFFED WITH CRAB IMPERIAL

Serves 8

8 boneless chicken breasts

- Preheat oven to 350°
- Place the chicken breasts in a greased casserole. Bake for 20 minutes. Remove from oven.
- Put crab meat on top of each breast.
- Bake for 15 minutes.
- Top with just a small amount of mayonnaise and sprinkle with paprika before serving.

*Crab Imperial*

| | |
|---|---|
| 2 pounds crab meat | 2 eggs |
| 1 tablespoon Dijon mustard | Juice of ½ lemon |
| 1 cup mayonnaise | 1 tsp. Worcestershire sauce |
| 1 teaspoon salt | ¼ teaspoon cayenne |
| 1 green pepper, chopped | ¼ teaspoon pepper |

- Combine all the ingredients except crab meat in a bowl. This can be covered and refrigerated until ready to use.

# CHICKEN A LA LEMON

Serves 6

6 boneless chicken breasts
Juice of 2 lemons
3 cloves garlic, minced
½ teaspoon salt
1 teaspoon fresh ground pepper
½ teaspoon thyme
½ teaspoon marjoram

½ teaspoon basil
1 teaspoon parsley
¼ cup flour
¼ cup panko
½ stick butter
Lemon slices
Cooked rice

- ♦ Marinate the chicken breasts in the lemon juice and garlic overnight.
- ♦ In a bowl combine all ingredients except butter, lemon slices and rice. Dip each breast in mixture. Place in baking dish
- ♦ Preheat oven to 400°
- ♦ Bake chicken in over for 45 minutes or until just browned.
- ♦ Serve with lemon slices and rice.

# STUFFED CHICKEN BREASTS

Serves 6

6 boneless chicken breasts
½ pound brie, sliced
½ pound crab meat

1 apple, sliced into 6 slices
½ stick butter, melted

- ♦ Preheat oven to 400°
- ♦ Pound the chicken breasts until thin. Place 1 slice of brie in center of breast. Top with crab meat and apple slice. Top with another piece of brie. Fold chicken together and secure with a toothpick.
- ♦ Place the chicken breast in a baking dish and top with butter.
- ♦ Bake ½ hour or until chicken is cooked. Do not overcook as it will be dry and cheese will melt.
- ♦ Serve with cranberry chutney.

# CHICKEN WITH PESTO CREAM SAUCE

Serves 6

6 boneless chicken breasts
6 slices bacon
6 large slices roasted red pepper

Asiago cheese, shaved
6 Tbls. butter

Preheat oven to 400°
Wrap the chicken breast with a roasted piece of pepper, shaved Asiago cheese, and bacon slice. Place in baking dish. Top with Tbls. butter. Bake ½ hour or until chicken is cooked. Serve with pesto cream sauce.

*Pesto Cream Sauce*

Pesto p. 201

½ cup heavy cream

Combine the ingredients in a bowl.


# CHICKEN AND OYSTERS

Serves 6

6 boneless chicken breasts

18 oysters

- ♦ Preheat oven to 350°
- ♦ Place the chicken breasts in a baking dish and bake ½ hour.
- ♦ Remove and top with oysters and Cream Sauce. Bake 15 minutes more.
- ♦ Serve hot with rice.

*Gruyere Cream Sauce*

1 stick butter
½ cup flour
1 ½ cups half and half

½ teaspoon nutmeg
½ pound Gruyere cheese

- ♦ Melt the butter in a sauce pan. Add the flour and stir in half until thickened. Stir in nutmeg and Gruyere.

# CHICKEN CASSEROLE

Serves 6

1 pound wide noodles
½ stick butter
¼ cup flour
1 ½ cups half and half
3 cups cooked chicken, cubed
½ red pepper, chopped
1 stalk celery, chopped

1 can sliced water chestnuts
¼ pound mushrooms, sliced
4 scallions, chopped
½ cup mayonnaise
1 cup cheddar cheese, grated
½ cup toasted almonds

- Preheat oven to 350°
- Cook the noodles according to directions. Drain and put in a greased casserole.
- In a sauce pan melt the butter, stir in flour and half and half.
- Remove from heat and stir in other ingredients, except almonds.
- Bake for ½ hour or until bubbly and just browned.
- Remove from oven and sprinkle with almonds.
- Tuna fish or turkey can be substituted for the chicken.
- If you're really in a hurry you can substitute a can of cream of mushroom or celery soup for the cream sauce.
- If you would like something spicier, substitute Monterrey Jack cheese for the cheddar cheese.

# EASY CHICKEN

Serves 6

6 boneless chicken breasts
½ pound mushrooms, sliced
¼ pound sun-dried tomatoes

1 large jar marinara sauce
1 cup parmesan cheese

- Preheat oven to 350°
- Place chicken in a baking dish. Top with mushrooms, tomatoes and marinara sauce. Sprinkle with cheese.
- Bake 45 minutes.

# CHICKEN WITH CAPER SAUCE

Serves 6

6 chicken boneless breasts          Juice of 1 lemon
¼ cup olive oil

- ♦ Combine the olive oil and lemon juice in a bowl. Roll the chicken
  breasts in the mixture. Grill the chicken breasts.

*Sundried Tomato Caper Relish*

½ pound sundried tomatoes,          ¼ cup olive oil
chopped                             ¼ cup capers

- ♦ Combine ingredients in a bowl. Serve with the chicken

# CHICKEN FRICASSEE

Serves 6-8

1 whole chicken, cut in pieces      3 cloves garlic, minced
1 stick butter                      ¼ cup parsley, chopped
¼ cup olive oil                     2 Tbls. dill, snipped
2 carrots, peeled and chopped       2 cups water
2 celery stalks, chopped            ¼ cup flour
1 leek, chopped                     ½ cup cream
½ pound mushrooms, sliced           ½ cup red wine

- ♦ Heat ½ stick butter with the olive oil in a Dutch oven or covered
  pot. Brown the chicken until golden.
- ♦ Add all the ingredients, except flour, cream and wine. Cover and
  bring to a boil. Simmer for 1 hour.
- ♦ In another pan heat ½ stick butter. Stir in flour, cream and wine
  until thickened. Slowly stir into large pot until thickened.
- ♦ Serve immediately with rice and garnish with fresh parsley.

# CHICKEN POT PIE

Serves 6

1 stick butter
½ cup flour
1 cup half and half
1 cup chicken broth
1 leeks diced
2 carrots, sliced

1 cup peas
1 cup lima beans
¼ cup fresh basil
Salt and pepper
3 cups cooked chicken breast, diced

- ◆ Preheat oven to 400°
- ◆ Melt the butter in a saucepan. Add flour and stir in milk and broth until thickened.
- ◆ Add rest of ingredients.
- ◆ Pour into 13" x 9" baking dish. Top with crust.
- ◆ Bake in oven for ½ hour or until top is just browned.

*Crust*

1 cup flour
1 stick butter
¼ cup milk

¼ teaspoon salt
3 Tbls. cream cheese

- ◆ Place all ingredients in food processor until ball forms.
- ◆ Roll out on floured board to the size of the baking dish.

# CHICKEN PESTO

Serves 6

6 boneless chicken breasts
Pesto p. 201

½ cup parmesan cheese

- ◆ Preheat oven to 350°
- ◆ Place the chicken breasts in a baking dish. Top with pesto and sprinkle with cheese.
- ◆ Bake 45 minutes.

# CHICKEN MARSALA

Serves 4

4 boneless chicken breasts
¼ cup flour
1 teaspoon dried basil
½ teaspoon dried oregano
½ stick butter

½ pound mushrooms
1 cup Marsala wine
Salt and pepper to taste
1 cup red currant jelly
1 cup sour cream

- ♦ Preheat oven to 350°
- ♦ Please flour and herbs in a bag. Shake breasts in flour.
- ♦ Heat the butter in a skillet and brown breasts.
- ♦ Pour Marsala over breasts and simmer for 10 minutes.
- ♦ Place breasts and Marsala in baking dish. Bake for 45 minutes.
- ♦ In a sauce pan melt the jelly and add sour cream. Stir in juices from chicken.
- ♦ Pour over chicken when ready to serve. Serve with noodles or rice.

# CHICKEN PICCATA

Serves 4

4 boneless chicken breasts, pounded thin
½ cup flour
½ teaspoon salt
½ teaspoon pepper
½ stick butter

½ cup white wine
Juice of 1 lemon
¼ cup capers
2 egg yolks
¼ cup fresh parsley, chopped
Lemon slices

- ♦ Combine the flour, salt and pepper in a paper bag. Roll the chicken breasts in flour mixture.
- ♦ Melt the butter in a skillet. Brown on all sides.
- ♦ Add the wine, lemon juice and capers. Simmer until tender, about 5 minutes. Remove meat from skillet and put on a serving dish.
- ♦ Add the egg yolks to the skillet until sauce is thickened. Pour over chicken. Garnish with lemon slices and parsley.
- ♦ Serve with rice or noodles.

# CHICKEN IN PINK CREAM SAUCE

Serves 6

½ stick butter
6 boneless chicken breasts
½ pound mushrooms

6 red peppers, cored and cut in half

- ♦ Preheat oven to broil
- ♦ Place the red peppers skin side up on a cookie sheet. Put under the broiler for 2-3 minutes, or until skins turn black.
- ♦ Transfer peppers to plastic bag. Seal and let sit 20 minutes. Remove from bag and peel off skin.
- ♦ Melt the butter in a skillet and brown chicken on all sides. Add mushrooms and peppers.
- ♦ Place chicken, mushrooms and peppers on a platter. Serve with Pink Cream sauce.

*Pink Cream Sauce*

½ stick butter
¼ cup flour
1½ cups cream

1 large tomato, finely chopped
¼ cup fresh basil

- ♦ In a sauce pan melt the butter. Stir in flour and cream. Add tomatoes and basil.

# SOUTHWESTERN CHICKEN

Serves 6

6 chicken breasts
2 large tomatoes chopped
2 green onions, sliced
3 cloves garlic, minced
2 jalapeno, chopped

¼ cup cilantro, chopped
1 teaspoon kosher salt
1 teaspoon fresh ground pepper
¼ cup olive oil

- ◆ Preheat oven to 350°
- ◆ In a bowl combine all ingredients. Place in baking dish. Bake for 45 minutes. Serve with rice.
- ◆ Chicken can also be grilled. Marinate for at least 4 hours in tomato mixture. Reserve mixture and serve over chicken after grilling.

# CURRIED CHICKEN

Serves 4

½ stick butter
1 small onion, chopped
4 cups diced cooked chicken
¼ cup flour
1 cup chicken stock
1 teaspoon Worcestershire sauce
¼ cup white wine
2 Tbls. tomato paste

½ teaspoon paprika
1 Tbls. curry
¼ teaspoon cayenne
¼ teaspoon cumin
½ teaspoon ground ginger
1 apple, cored and sliced
½ cup raisins

- ◆ Melt the butter in a skillet. Add onion. Stir until translucent. Add chicken. Stir in flour and stock. Add other ingredients.
- ◆ Serve over rice.
- ◆ Condiments should include chutney, raisins, peanuts, chopped egg, coconut and mashed bananas.

# CHICKEN SALTIMBOCCA

Serves 6

6 boneless chicken breasts, pounded thinly
½ cup flour
½ teaspoon salt
½ teaspoon pepper
½ stick butter

6 slices prosciutto
½ pound of Fontina cheese, shaved
6 fresh sage leaves
½ cup dry white wine

- Preheat oven to 375°
- In a wide bowl combine the flour, salt and pepper. Dredge the chicken in the flour.
- Melt ½ of butter in a skillet. Brown chicken breasts.
- Place breasts in a baking dish. Put a piece of the cheese, 1 slice of prosciutto and a sage leaf on each breast. Roll up and faster with a toothpick.
- Add the wine to the skillet. Cook until reduced by ½. Add butter. Pour over chicken.
- Place in oven and bake for 15 minutes, or until chicken is thoroughly warmed.
- Serve immediately with pasta

# BRAISED CHICKEN

Serves 6

½ stick butter
1 small onion, chopped
3 carrots, chopped
1 chicken, cut up
¼ cup flour
½ cup dry white wine

½ cup chicken broth
1 teaspoon kosher salt
1 teaspoon fresh ground pepper
1 bunch watercress, stems removed and chopped

- Preheat oven to 350°
- Melt the butter in a Dutch oven. Add onion and carrots. Saute for 5 minutes. Add chicken and brown. Add other ingredients. Cover.
- Bake in oven for 1 hour, or until chicken is tender.

# CHICKEN DIVAN

Serves 4

1 pound fresh broccoli florets          4 boneless chicken breasts

- Preheat oven to 350°
- Blanche the broccoli. Place in greased baking dish. Top with chicken and sauce.
- Bake for 45 minutes, or until bubbling and just browned.
- Serve with rice.

*White Sauce*

½ stick butter                    ½ teaspoon salt
¼ cup flour                       1 teaspoon pepper
1½ cups half and half             ½ pound Gruyere
½ teaspoon nutmeg                 ¼ cup Sherry

- Melt the butter in a sauce pan. Stir in flour and half and half until thickened. Add other ingredients.


# CHICKEN TAGINE

Serves 6

1 whole chicken, cut into pieces       2 tomatoes, chopped
1 medium onion, chopped                ½ cup red pepper, chopped
3 cloves garlic, minced                ½ cup yellow pepper, chopped
½ teaspoon tumeric                     2 large carrots, peeled and
1 teaspoon cinnamon                    chopped
½ teaspoon ginger                      ½ cup raisins
½ teaspoon nutmeg                      ¼ cup almonds
½ teaspoon cayenne                     ½ pound dried apricots
½ teaspoon cloves                      ¼ pound dates
2 cups water                           1 cup uncooked couscous

- Preheat oven to 350°
- Put all ingredients in covered baking dish.
- Bake 1 hour or until chicken is tender.

# BAKED CHICKEN

Serves 4

4 boneless chicken breasts
1 teaspoon garlic salt
1 Tbls. chili powder
Juice of 1 lemon
1 teaspoon fresh ground pepper

1 teaspoon kosher salt
½ teaspoon cayenne
1 teaspoon cumin
1 cup sour cream

- ♦ Preheat oven to 500°
- ♦ Combine all ingredients in a bowl, except chicken.
- ♦ Place the chicken breasts in a baking dish. Pour the sour cream sauce over the chicken.
- ♦ Bake for 15 minutes and then turn oven to 350°. Bake for ½ more.
- ♦ Serve with basmati rice and chutney.

# CHICKEN STEW

Serves 6-8

1 whole chicken, cut into pieces
½ pound mushrooms, sliced
1 red pepper, chopped
1 yellow pepper, chopped
1 cup pitted black olives
4 large tomatoes, chopped
4 slices bacon, chopped
½ cup white wine
2 stalks celery, chopped

1 medium onion, chopped
2 carrots, sliced
3 cloves garlic, minced
2 cups water
1 teaspoon salt
1 teaspoon fresh ground pepper
½ teaspoon cayenne
1 Tbls. dried tarragon or basil
1 cup rice

- ♦ Preheat oven to 350°
- ♦ Combine all ingredients in Dutch oven. Cover and cook for 1½ hours, until meat is falling off bones. Bones can be removed for easier eating.

# CHICKEN STEW

Serves 4

2 large boneless chicken breasts,
cut in half
1 medium onion, chopped
1 red pepper, chopped
1 carrot, sliced
1 jalapeno, chopped

3 cloves garlic, minced
2 Tbls. fresh grated ginger
½ cup dark rum
2 Tbls. soy sauce
½ stick butter, melted

- ♦ Preheat oven to 350°
- ♦ Combine all ingredients in a Dutch oven.
- ♦ Bake 1 hour. Stir every 15 minutes.
- ♦ Serve with rice.


# CHICKEN STEW

This is a hearty one dish meal.

Serves 6

1 whole chicken, cut into pieces
1 teaspoon oregano
1 teaspoon dried coriander
1 teaspoon curry
½ teaspoon cayenne
2 cups water
2 tomatoes, chopped
1 medium onion, chopped

3 cloves garlic, minced
1 cup uncooked rice
1 cup fresh or frozen peas
½ cup green pepper, chopped
½ cup red pepper, chopped
1 cup ham, diced
1 cup green or black olives
2 Tbls. capers

- ♦ Preheat oven to 350°
- ♦ Combine all ingredients in a large covered Dutch oven. Bake 1 ½ hours until chicken is falling off bones.
- ♦ Remove from oven and remove bones. Bake for 15 minutes more, until steaming hot.
- ♦ Serve in bowls with crusty bread.

# CHICKEN STEW

Serves 6

6 boneless chicken breasts
½ teaspoon salt
1 teaspoon pepper
½ stick butter, melted
1 medium onion, chopped

3 cloves garlic, minced
3 tomatoes, chopped
1 cup white wine
½ cup black olives
¼ cup parsley, chopped

- ◆ Preheat oven to 350°
- ◆ Combine all the ingredients in a Dutch oven.
- ◆ Bake 1 hour
- ◆ Serve with rice.
- ◆ 1 cup uncooked rice and 2 cups wine can be cooked with chicken for a one dish meal.

# CHICKEN PAPRIKA

Serves 12

1 cup flour
1 Tbls. paprika
¼ teaspoon cayenne
½ teaspoon ginger
¼ cup fresh basil, chopped
½ teaspoon nutmeg
½ teaspoon cloves
1 teaspoon kosher salt
1 teaspoon fresh ground pepper

2 chickens, cut into parts
1 stick butter
1 medium onion, chopped
6 cloves garlic, minced
3 cups water
2 cups sour cream
1 Tbls. Worcestershire sauce
½ cup Sherry

- ◆ Preheat oven to 350°
- ◆ In a paper back combine the flour and spices. Shake the chicken pieces, a few at a time in the bag.
- ◆ In a large skillet melt ½ the butter. Brown the chicken pieces. Add the onion and garlic.
- ◆ Put the chicken in a large baking dish.
- ◆ In a bowl combine the water, sour cream, Worcestershire and sherry. Pour over the chicken.
- ◆ Bake 1 hour, or until chicken is tender.
- ◆ Serve with cooked noodles.

# CHICKEN CASSEROLE

Serves 6

1 ½ cups uncooked wild rice
½ stick butter
3 green onions, chopped
½ pound mushrooms, sliced
3 cups chicken broth
6 boneless chicken breasts
½ yellow pepper, chopped

½ red pepper, chopped
¼ cup parsley, chopped
½ teaspoon salt
1 teaspoon pepper
½ cup toasted almonds
½ cup white wine

- ♦ Preheat oven to 350°
- ♦ Combine all ingredients in covered Dutch oven or casserole for 1 hour.

# ROAST TURKEY

1 20 pound turkey

- ♦ Preheat oven to 350°
- ♦ Stuff turkey and place in roasting pan.
- ♦ Cook covered for 5 hours (15 minutes per pound)

*Sausage Stuffing*

1 stick butter
½ pound ham sausage
1 leek, chopped
½ pound mushrooms
2 large apples, peeled, cored and chopped

1 loaf herb bread, cubed
1 cup pecans
1 teaspoon sage
1 teaspoon thyme
1 teaspoon rosemary
Salt and pepper

- ♦ Melt the butter in large skillet. Add the leeks, mushrooms, sausage and apples. Add the bread and cook until just browned. Add pecans and seasonings.

# ROAST DUCK

Serves 4

1 5-6 pound duckling                    Salt and pepper
½ stick butter, softened

- ♦ Preheat oven to 500°
- ♦ Rub the duck with the softened butter. Sprinkle salt and pepper on duck. Place in baking dish.
- ♦ Roast for 20-25 or until browned. Reduce heat to 350°. Bake for 25 more minutes.
- ♦ Serve with apricot or orange sauce – p. 204, 205

# DUCK A L'ORANGE

Serves 8

2 5 - pound ducks                 2 carrots, chopped
1 medium onion, chopped      Salt and pepper
2 stalks celery, chopped

- ♦ Preheat oven to 500°
- ♦ Rinse and pat dry the ducks. Divide the vegetables between the 2 duck cavities. Sprinkle duck with salt and pepper.
- ♦ Put in roasting pan and bake 20 minutes. Reduce heat to 350°. Cook for 1 hour.
- ♦ Remove from oven and place on serving platter.
- ♦ Serve with Grand Marnier Sauce - p. 206

# STUFFED CORNISH HENS

Serves 4

4 small Cornish hens

- ◆ Preheat oven to 500°
- ◆ Place the Cornish hens in a baking dish. Stuff each with stuffing.
- ◆ Bake 15 minutes. Turn oven to 350°. Bake for 30 minutes more.

*Stuffing*

½ stick butter
1 medium onion, chopped
2 stalks celery, chopped
¼ cup fresh parsley, chopped
1 cup cooked wild rice

1 cup cooked basmati rice
½ cup slivered almonds
½ pound mushrooms, sliced
4 slices bacon, cooked and crumbled

- ◆ Melt the butter in a skillet. Add onion and celery. Cook 5 minutes. Add other ingredients.

# STUFFED CORNISH HENS

Serves 4

4 small Cornish hens

*Dressing*

1 stick butter
2 cups white bread, cubed
1 cup raisins
1 cup pecans

1 cup dried apricots, chopped
2 Tbls. fresh grated ginger
2 Tbls. orange juice
2 Tbls. orange zest

- ◆ Preheat oven to 500°
- ◆ Melt the butter in a skillet. Add bread and just lightly toast. Add other ingredients.
- ◆ Stuff Cornish hens with dressing. Place in baking dish and dot hens with butter and sprinkle with kosher salt.
- ◆ Roast for 20 minutes. Reduce heat to 350°. Baste hens.
- ◆ Cook for 30 minutes or until hens are tender.

# ROAST GOOSE

Serves 6

1 6-8 pound goose                    Kosher salt

- ◆ Preheat oven to 400°
- ◆ Put goose in baking dish. Rub goose with salt. Stuff goose.
- ◆ Bake for 3 hours.

*Stuffing*

½ stick butter                      ½ teaspoon thyme
1 small onion, chopped              ½ teaspoon salt
1 apple, cored and diced            ½ teaspoon pepper
1 stalk celery, chopped             ¼ cup pecans
2 cups herb bread                   ¼ cup dates, raisins or prunes
½ teaspoon sage                     ¼ cup orange juice

- ◆ Melt the butter in a skillet. Add onion, apple and celery. Cook for 5 minutes. Add the other ingredients.

# TURKEY CURRY

Serves 4

½ stick butter                      1 cup chicken stock
1 small onion, chopped              ½ cup coconut milk
1 apple, cored and sliced           1 Tbls. curry powder
1 celery stalk, sliced              1 teaspoon ground ginger
4 cups turkey                       ¼ teaspoon cayenne
¼ cup flour                         ½ teaspoon cumin
                                    Juice of 1 lemon

- ◆ Melt the butter in a skillet. Stir in onion, apple, and celery. Cook for 5 minutes. Add turkey and flour. Stir in stock and coconut milk. Add spices.
- ◆ Serve over rice with condiments such as raisins, coconut, chopped hardboiled eggs, chutney, bananas, and macadamia nuts.

# MEATS

The author's grandparents Col. and Mrs. Grafton Kennedy, her parents
Kay and Bill Barney, and aunt Lou Albert enjoy a summer afternoon in
the 1950's.

The early settlers in the Chesapeake region ate deer, muskrat, squirrel, and other wild animals. Muskrat is still served and often used in Brunswick stew.

The soil in Virginia was not good for growing tobacco which was to become the major crop of the South and in Maryland also. Instead farmers turned to raising pigs. Virginia hams are known worldwide for their delicious flavor and smokiness. Hogs ate snakes, nuts, and anything they could get hold of. The earliest pigs were brought from England and Bermuda shortly after the settlement of Jamestown in 1607. By 1639 pork and bacon were being shipped to New England.

Virginia hams are salted, smoked and then aged. The most famous are from Smithfield. By an act of the legislature pigs were permitted to be called Smithfield. The pigs are raised in Virginia and North Carolina. The pigs are fed a diet of corn and peanuts for the first six months. They must then be cured, treated, smoked and processed in Smithfield. The hams are known for their saltiness. They must be scrubbed, washed and baked to remove some of this. The ham is served sliced very thin on biscuits or in dishes such as scrambled eggs and in soup where the bone is also cooked. The hams are traditionally served at Christmas, but can be used any time of the year.

Hams can be cured at home using a mixture of salt and sugar and kept at a temperature of 36° for 1 ½ days per pound. Once cured they are soaked in water and then stored for 2 weeks. The ham is then smoked using hickory or other chips. They are then aged for at least 7 weeks.

# BEEF TOURNEDOS WITH OYSTERS

Serves 6

½ pound fresh baby spinach
2 Tbls. butter
2 dozen oysters

2 ½ pounds beef tenderloin,
sliced into six pieces
Bearnaise Sauce – p.202

- ◆ Preheat the oven to 350°. Place the oysters on a cookie sheet and bake until opened. Remove oysters from shells.
- ◆ In a skillet melt the butter and sauté the spinach until wilted. Stir in the oysters.
- ◆ Heat broiler.
- ◆ Place the beef in a broiler pan, and place under broiler for 4 minutes to side. Remove from heat.
- ◆ Serve with spinach and oysters on top. Pour Bearnaise sauce over the mixture. Serve immediately.
- ◆ Crab can be substituted for the oysters.

# STEAK AU POIVRE

Serves 6

2½ pounds boneless sirloin steak
¼ cup whole black peppercorns,
coarsely crushed

3 Tbls. kosher salt

- ◆ Rub the salt into the steak. Sprinkle the peppercorns on both sides of the steak, pressing them into the meat.
- ◆ Grill the steak on a BBQ until desired pinkness.
- ◆ Serve with Sherry Mustard Cream Sauce.

*Sherry Mustard Cream Sauce*

½ cup sour cream
½ cup heavy cream

3 Tbls. Dijon mustard
¼ cup dry Sherry

- ◆ Beat the cream in a bowl until peaks form. Fold in other ingredients.

# STEAK AU POIVRE II

Serves 6

2 ½ pounds sirloin steak
¼ cup whole green/pink peppers, coarsely crushed
2 Tbls. kosher salt
½ stick butter

¼ cup flour
1 cup heavy cream
¼ cup Cognac
2 Tbls. shallots, chopped
Parsley

- ♦ Rub the steak with the peppercorns and salt, pressing them into the meat.
- ♦ In a large skillet braise the steak on both sides to desired pinkness.
- ♦ Remove from skillet and place in 200° oven on a platter.
- ♦ Melt the butter in the skillet with the steak drippings. Add flour and cream until slightly thickened. Add Cognac and shallots.
- ♦ Pour the Cognac cream over steak. Garnish with parsley.

# STEAK WITH HERB BUTTER

Serves 6

2½ pounds boneless sirloin steak
2 Tbls. fresh ground pepper
1 Tbls. garlic salt

1 Tbls. kosher salt
½ teaspoon cayenne

- ♦ Rub the steak with the salt, pepper, garlic, and cayenne.
- ♦ Grill the steak on a BBQ until desired pinkness (or redness)
- ♦ Serve with herb butter

*Herb Butter*

1 stick butter, room temperature
½ cup parsley, chopped
2 shallots, chopped
2 cloves garlic, chopped

½ cup fresh basil, chopped
½ teaspoon kosher salt
½ teaspoon fresh ground pepper
¼ cup lemon juice

- ♦ Combine all the ingredients in a bowl. Roll into 6 balls. Put in freezer for 15 minutes. Place a ball on each steak after steaks are grilled.

# BEEF STROGANOFF

Serves 6

½ stick butter
½ pound mushrooms, sliced
2 dozen baby onions
2 ½ pounds beef tenderloin, cut into small strips
3 cloves garlic, minced

3 Tbls. flour
1 cup beef broth
2 Tbls. tomato paste
8 ounces sour cream
½ cup Sherry

- In a skillet melt the butter and add mushrooms and onions, sautéing until just tender.
- Reserve liquid in skillet and put mushrooms and onions in a bowl. Add meat to skillet. Just brown.
- Stir in garlic and flour. Add beef broth and tomato paste. Stir in mushrooms, onions and beef. Add sherry and sour cream.
- Serve over noodles.

# BEEF TENDERLOIN

Serves 6

2 ½ pounds beef tenderloin, cut in 6 pieces
¼ cup fresh ground pepper
2 Tbls. salt

½ stick butter
¾ pound mushrooms
½ cup Port
½ pound Stilton cheese

- Rub the tenderloins with the pepper and salt.
- Grill the beef on a BBQ until desired pinkness.
- In a skillet melt the butter and sauté the mushrooms for 3 minutes. Add Port.
- Place the tenderloins on a platter or individual plates. Pour the mushrooms over top.
- Sprinkle some of the cheese over each tenderloin.

# STEAK WITH CARMELIZED ONIONS

Serves 6

2 ½ pounds sirloin
2 Tbls. pepper
1 Tbls. salt
½ stick butter
3 large onions, sliced

1 Tbls. sugar
1 teaspoon salt
3 cloves garlic, minced
¼ cup basil, chopped

- ♦ Melt the butter in a skillet. Add onions. Cover and cook for 15 minutes, stirring occasionally. Uncover and raise heat. Add sugar and salt. Cook for 15 more minutes.
- ♦ Rub the pepper and salt into the steak. Grill steak on BBQ until desired pinkness.
- ♦ Place on platter and cover with onions.


# BEEF STEW

Serves 6

2 Tbls. olive oil
2½ pounds stewing beef, cut into 1 inch pieces
1 onion, chopped
6 red bliss potatoes, cubed
½ red bell pepper, chopped
½ yellow pepper, chopped
3 cloves garlic, minced
2 bay leaves
¼ cup cilantro, chopped

1 cup peas
1 cup black olives
1 teaspoon oregano
¼ cup parsley, chopped
3 tomatoes, chopped
3 carrots, peeled and sliced
1 Tbls. curry
3 cups water
Juice of 1 lemon
½ cup dark rum

- ♦ Heat the olive oil in a Dutch oven and add meat. Cook until just browned.
- ♦ Add other ingredients except rum. Cover.
- ♦ Cook on low heat for 1½ hours, stirring occasionally.
- ♦ Add rum just before serving.
- ♦ Stew can also be baked in 325°.

# LASAGNA

Serves 4

1 pound ground meat
1 medium onion,
1 15 ounce can crushed tomatoes
1 small can tomato paste
3 cloves garlic, minced
1 Tbls. Italian herbs

1 teaspoon chili powder
¼ cup basil, chopped
Salt, pepper to taste
½ pound wide noodles, cooked according to instructions
1 cup shredded mozzarella cheese

- ◆ Preheat oven to 350°
- ◆ In a skillet saute ground beef and onions until meat is just browned. Add tomatoes, garlic, herbs, chili, basil and salt and pepper.
- ◆ Place the noodles in a baking dish. Cover with filling, then meat mixture.
- ◆ Sprinkle the cheese on top.
- ◆ Bake for 35 minutes or until bubbling.

*Filling*

1 cup sour cream
1 8 oz. package cream cheese

4 green onions, sliced

- ◆ Combine ingredients in a bowl.

# BURGERS

Serves 4

1½ pounds ground beef
2 green onions, chopped
4 Tbls. blue cheese

2 cloves garlic, minced
4 rolls

- ◆ Make the beef into 4 patties. Make a hole in each and stuff with blue cheese, onion and garlic.
- ◆ Grill on a BBQ until desired pinkness.
- ◆ Serve on rolls with condiments.

# CHILI CASSEROLE

Serves 6

2 Tbls. olive oil
½ cup red pepper, chopped
1 small onion, chopped
3 cloves garlic, minced
2 jalapenos, chopped
1 pound ground beef
1 Tbls. chili powder
½ teaspoon cumin

1 15 oz. can tomato sauce
1 cup corn
2 cups shredded cheddar cheese
3 green onion, chopped
¼ cup chopped pitted black olives

- ◆ Preheat oven to 400°
- ◆ In a large skillet heat the olive oil and sauté the pepper and onion. Add the garlic, jalapenos and beef. Stir in chili, cumin and tomato sauce.
- ◆ Pour into 9x13 inch baking dish. Sprinkle with corn and cheddar cheese, then topping, olives and green onions.
- ◆ Bake 30 minutes, or until just browned and bubbling. Serve hot.

*Topping*

2 eggs
1 cup milk
½ cup flour

1 cup cornmeal
1 Tbls. olive oil

- ◆ Beat all ingredients in a bowl until smooth. Pour over casserole.

# CHILI POTATOES

Serves 6

Chili – see next recipe
 6 baking potatoes

2 cups mozzarella cheese, grated
6 green onions, chopped

- ◆ Preheat oven to 400°
- ◆ Cook potatoes in microwave 10 minutes. Cut in half lengthwise
- ◆ Spread some of the chili on each potato half. Top with cheese and onion. Bake in oven about 12 minutes and cheese melts.

# CHILI

Serves 8

2 Tbls. olive oil
1 large onion, chopped
1 red bell pepper, chopped
1 yellow pepper, chopped
4 large ripe tomatoes, chopped
3 jalapeno, seeded and chopped
2 ½ pounds ground beef
½ pound sausage
4 cloves garlic, minced
4 slices bacon, cooked and chopped

1 teaspoon salt
½ teaspoon cayenne
1 Tbls. chili powder
1 Tbls. Italian herbs
Sour Cream
Grated cheddar cheese
3 green onions, chopped
Guacamole, p. 200
Salsa, p. 199
Tortilla chips

- ◆ Heat the olive oil in a pot. Stir in onion, peppers, tomatoes and jalapeno. Remove and put in a bowl.
- ◆ Put the ground beef and sausage in the pot. Brown. Add garlic, bacon, salt, cayenne, chili and herbs. Stir in tomato sauce.
- ◆ Serve in bowls and garnish with sour cream, grated cheese, and green onions. Serve guacamole, salsa and chips on side.

# CURRIED LAMB

Serves 4

½ stick butter
1 small onion, chopped
3 cloves garlic, minced
¼ cup flour
1½ cups chicken stock
1 teaspoon cinnamon
¼ teaspoon ground cloves

1 Tbls. curry
½ teaspoon paprika
½ teaspoon cumin
1 teaspoon coriander
2 tbls. fresh grated ginger
4 cups cooked lamb
2 cups cooked rice

- ◆ Melt butter in a skillet and cook onion until transparent. Stir in garlic, flour and stock until just slightly thickened. Stir in other ingredients, except rice.
- ◆ Serve over rice with condiments such as chutney, coconut, and nuts.

113

# CURRIED LAMB

Serves 4

½ stick butter
1 small onion, chopped
2 cloves garlic, minced
¼ cup flour
1½ cups chicken stock
4 cups cooked boneless lamb

½ cup applesauce
½ cup red wine
3 tbls fresh grated ginger
1 Tbls. curry
½ pound mushrooms, sliced
2 cups cooked rice

- Melt butter in a skillet and sauté onion until transparent.
- Add garlic, flour and stock until thickened. Stir in other ingredients.
- Serve with chopped crystallized ginger, coconut, chopped green pepper, peanuts, chopped egg, chutney

# SKEWERED LAMB

Serves 6

¼ cup olive oil
¼ cup lemon juice
1 Tbls. kosher salt
1 Tbls. pepper
1 Tbls. oregano
2½ pounds boneless lamb, cut in
1 inch cubes

Skewers
3 red bliss potatoes, cubed
2 large onions, cubed
1 red bell pepper, cubed
1 yellow pepper, cubed

- In a bowl combine the olive oil, lemon juice, salt, pepper and oregano. Add the lamb. Marinate for at least two hours.
- Alternate the lamb and vegetables on skewers.
- Grill on BBQ and 5 minutes to a side. Baste with remaining marinade.
- Serve with fresh oregano, lemon slices and rice.

# RACK OF LAMB

Serves 6

3 pounds rack of lamb, trimmed
1 Tbls. kosher salt
1 Tbls. fresh ground pepper
2 Tbls. chives
2 Tbls. parsley

2 shallots, chopped
2 cloves garlic, minced
¼ cup olive oil
½ stick butter
1 cup bread crumbs

- ♦ Preheat oven to 450°
- ♦ In a bowl combine all ingredients, except lamb.
- ♦ Place the lamb in a baking dish and coat with breadcrumb mixture.
- ♦ Cook 30 minutes, or lamb is just pink.
- ♦ Can also be used with crown roast of pork

# MARINATED LEG OF LAMB

Serves 8

3 ½ pound boneless leg of lamb
¼ cup Dijon mustard
¼ cup olive oil
2 Tbls. lemon juice

4 cloves garlic, grated
2 Tbls.rosemary
1 Tbls. fresh ground pepper

- ♦ In a bowl combine the mustard, olive oil, garlic, rosemary and pepper.
- ♦ Rub the lamb with the marinade.
- ♦ Cook on grill about 25 minutes to a side, until just pink.
- ♦ Serve with horseradish sauce.

# LAMB STEW

Serves 4-6

2 cups water
2 pounds lamb, cubed
2 carrots, chopped
1 large onion, chopped
2 turnips, peeled and chopped
4 medium potatoes, peeled and chopped

2 stalks celery, chopped
1 leek, chopped
1 cup cabbage, shredded
1 Tbls. Worcestershire sauce
1 cup cream
Parsley

- ♦ Place all ingredients except for cream in large pot. Bring to a boil. Simmer for 1 hour or until meat and vegetables are tender.
- ♦ Add cream. Serve in bowls and garnish with parsley.

# VEAL

Serves 6

1½ pounds veal scaloppini (6 large slices)
¼ teaspoon dried sage
½ teaspoon fresh ground pepper
6 slices prosciutto

¼ pound mozzarella, sliced
½ stick butter
2 Tbls. flour
½ cup dry white wine

- ♦ Preheat oven to 325°
- ♦ Sprinkle each slice of veal with sage and pepper. Place prosciutto and mozzarella slices on each piece of veal. Roll veal up and fasten with a toothpick.
- ♦ Heat butter in a skillet. Cook veal until just browned on all sides. Remove from heat. Place in baking dish.
- ♦ Stir flour into veal dripping. Add wine. Pour over veal.
- ♦ Bake ½ hour.

# VEAL MARSALA

Serves 4

2 Tbls. butter
1 pound veal scaloppini, 4 large
slices
1 teaspoon pepper
1 teaspoon sage

1 teaspoon oregano
¼ pound prosciutto, sliced
¼ pound Gruyere
2 Tbls. flour
¼ cup Marsala

- ◆ Preheat oven to 350°
- ◆ Melt the butter in an iron skillet. Just slightly brown each veal slice on both sides. Remove from skillet. Sprinkle some pepper, sage and oregano on each slice.
- ◆ Place 1 piece of prosciutto on each scaloppini and a small amount of Gruyere. Roll up scaloppini and fasten with toothpick. Place back in skillet and warm in oven for 10 minutes. Remove veal.
- ◆ Add flour and stir in Marsala.
- ◆ Put veal on a platter and pour Marsala sauce over veal.
- ◆ Serve with pasta.

# GRILLED VEAL CHOPS

Serves 6

6 loin veal chops
¼ cup white wine
¼ cup lemon juice
2 Tbls. rosemary

3 cloves garlic, minced
1 Tbls. kosher salt
1 Tbls. pepper

- ◆ In a bowl marinate all ingredients for at least 2 hours.
- ◆ Grill on BBQ until veal is just pink.
- ◆ Serve with oregano and lemon slices.

# VEAL CHOPS

Serves 6

6 loin veal chops
¼ pound prosciutto

¼ pound fontina cheese
1 Tbls. sage

- ♦ Preheat oven to 350°
- ♦ Stuff each veal chop with some prosciutto, cheese and sage.
- ♦ Bake ½ hour. Serve with wild mushroom brandy sauce

Wild Mushroom Brandy Sauce

½ stick butter
½ pound wild mushrooms, chopped

¼ cup flour
1 cup cream
¼ cup brandy

- ♦ Melt the butter in a sauce pan. Stir in mushrooms and flour. Add cream until just slightly thickened. Stir in brandy.

# VENISON STROGANOFF

Serves 6

½ stick butter
2 ½ pounds boneless venison steak, cut in 1 inch strips
¾ pound mushrooms
1 leek, sliced
3 cloves garlic, minced
2 cups beef broth
½ cup tomato paste

1 teaspoon rosemary
2 bay leaves
2 Tbls. parsley, chopped
½ cup red wine
1 cup sour cream
1 pound wide noodles, cooked according to directions

- ♦ Melt the butter in a skillet and brown venison on each side. Remove meat. Add mushrooms and leeks. Cook 3 minutes.
- ♦ Add garlic, broth, tomato paste, rosemary, bay and parsley. Bring to a boil.
- ♦ Stir in red wine and sour cream. Add meat.
- ♦ Serve with noodles.

# PORK TENDERLOIN WITH APPLE SAUCE

Serves 8

3½ pound boneless pork tenderloin

4 apples, peeled, cored and sliced

2 large onions, peeled and sliced

½ stick butter

½ cup sugar

¼ cup cider

- ♦ This is a very pretty and delicious fall dish.
- ♦ Preheat oven to 350°. In a roasting pan cook the pork until desired pinkness, about 1½ hours. Remove from pan and place on a platter.
- ♦ In the roasting pan heat the onions, butter and sugar until the onions are carmelized about 10 minutes. Stir in the apples and cider. Serve over the pork.
- ♦ The pork can also be baked with the other ingredients, but be careful that they do not burn on the sides of pan. Baste during the baking.

# PORK TENDERLOIN

Serves 6

2½ pounds pork tenderloin

¼ cup Dijon mustard

1 cup breadcrumbs

3 cloves garlic, minced

1 Tbls. sage

1 Tbls. oregano

1 Tbls. rosemary

2 Tbls. fresh ground pepper

1 Tbls. kosher salt

- ♦ Preheat oven to 350°
- ♦ Combine all the ingredients in a bowl. Place in a baking pan.
- ♦ Bake for 1 hour.
- ♦ Serve with horseradish sauce.

# CHICKEN AND HAM CROQUETTES

Makes 6 croquettes

2 Tbls. butter
2 Tbls. flour
½ cup half and half
1 egg, beaten
1 teaspoon Worcestershire sauce
Dash of Tabasco

2 green onions, chopped
2 Tbls. fresh tarragon, chopped
1 cup ham, ground
1 cup cooked chicken, ground
1 cup Italian bread crumbs
Vegetable oil

♦ In a sauce pan melt the butter and stir in flour. Pour the half and half in slowly until thickened. Remove from heat. Stir in egg. Add Worcestershire and Tabasco sauces. Fold in green onion, tarragon, ham and chicken.
♦ Divide mixture into 6 portions. Shape into croquette or ball. Roll in bread crumbs.
♦ Pour vegetable oil into skillet.
♦ Fry the croquettes until browned on all sides.
♦ Arrange on platter. Serve with chive sauce.

*Chive Sauce*

½ stick butter
¼ cup flour
1 ½ cups half and half

¼ cup dry white wine
1 Tbls. tarragon
¼ cup chives, snipped

♦ In a sauce pan melt the butter. Stir in flour and add milk until thickened. Stir in white wine. Add tarragon and chives.

# HAM CROQUETTES

Makes 6 croquettes

2 eggs
2 cups ham
1 cup bread crumbs
1 small onion, chopped

½ cup milk
2 Tbls. parsley, chopped
2 chopped hardboiled eggs

♦ In a bowl combine all the ingredients. Shape into balls. Heat vegetable oil in a skillet. Drop balls into oil and just brown.

# VEGETABLES

Vegetables and Dip

*"You needn't tell me that a man who doesn't love oysters and asparagus and good wines has got a soul, or a stomach either. He's simply got the instinct for being unhappy."*
'Saki', pen name of Scottish writer Hector Hugh Munro (1870-1916)


Thomas Jefferson introduced French Fries to America during his presidency at the White House (1801-09)

Even though Thomas Jefferson's Monticello is inland in Charlottesville, we are thankful to him for bringing Belgian endive, eggplant, salsify, and artichokes from Europe to plant in his garden.


# TOMATO PATTIES

Serves 6

4 large tomatoes, peeled and finely chopped
2 medium onions, finely chopped
¼ cup fresh mint, chopped

¼ cup fresh parsley, chopped
Salt and pepper
¼ cup flour
¼ cup olive oil

- ◆ In a bowl combine the tomatoes, onions, mint, parsley, salt and pepper to taste. Add flour.
- ◆ Shape into patties.
- ◆ Heat the olive oil in a skillet and add tomato patties, a few at a time. Brown on both sides.
- ◆ Serve hot.
- ◆ Grated parmesan cheese can be added for extra flavor to the patties.

# TOMATO AND ONION TART

Serves 4

*Pastry*

1¼ cups flour                       ¼ cup cold water
1 stick butter                      3 Tbls. cream cheese

- ♦ Preheat the oven to 400°
- ♦ Blend all the ingredients in a food processor. Roll into pie crust shape and place in pie plate.
- ♦ Bake for 10 minutes. Remove from oven.

*Filling*

½ stick butter                      2 large tomatoes, thinly sliced
1 pound sweet onion, such as        ¼ cup fresh basil, chopped
Vidalia, peeled and sliced          3 eggs
1 cup Gruyere cheese, grated        1 ½ cups half and half

- ♦ Melt the butter in a skillet and add onions cooking until just tender.
- ♦ Spread the tomatoes evenly over the crust. Top with basil, onions and then cheese.
- ♦ In a bowl beat the eggs and half and half. Pour over the pie mixture.
- ♦ Place in oven and bake for 35 minutes or until golden.

# ROASTED VEGETABLES

Serves 8

1 large eggplant, sliced            2 Tbls. kosher salt
1 red bell pepper, sliced           1 Tbls. rosemary
1 yellow pepper, sliced             1 teaspoon thyme
1 pound portabella mushrooms,
sliced
¼ cup olive oil

Preheat oven to 400°
Place all ingredients in a baking dish. Bake for 45 minutes.

# BAKED EGGPLANT

Serves 4

2 pounds eggplant, peeled and sliced
4 Tbls. olive oil
fresh basil

½ pound Mozzarella, shredded
4 cloves garlic, minced
1 15 oz. can tomato sauce
1 cup parmesan cheese

- ♦ Preheat broiler
- ♦ Brush eggplant slices with olive oil and place on cookie sheet. Put under broiler until just browned 3-4 minutes. Turn eggplant and brown on other side.
- ♦ Preheat over to 350°
- ♦ Combine all ingredients, except eggplant and parmesan cheese. Spoon onto eggplant slices. Top with parmesan cheese.
- ♦ Bake for 20 minutes.


# FRIED EGGPLANT

Serves 6

1 large eggplant, cut in half lengthwise, with each half cut in 12 pieces
1 Tbls. kosher salt
1 cup flour

1 teaspoon cumin
¼ teaspoon red pepper
½ cup cold water
2 eggs
Vegetable oil

- ♦ Place the eggplant in a large bowl and sprinkle with salt.
- ♦ In another bowl combine the flour, cumin, red pepper, eggs and water.
- ♦ Pour the vegetable oil into a large skillet. Heat the oil, but do not let splatter.
- ♦ Dip the eggplant into the batter. Fry the eggplant in the hot oil, until browned on both sides.
- ♦ Transfer to a dish lined with paper towels.
- ♦ Serve warm with tomato sauce or salsa.

# VEGETABLE SAMOSAS

Phyllo pastry sheets, cut into squares

*Filling*

¼ cup olive oil
1 large Vidalia onion, peeled and chopped finely
2 cloves garlic, minced
2 jalapeno, seeded and chopped
4 green onions, chopped
2 large baking potatoes, boiled, peeled and mashed

1 teaspoon curry powder
¼ cup cilantro, chopped
¼ cup tomato sauce
1 cup fresh baby spinach, finely chopped
½ cup peas
Juice of ½ lemon

- ◆ Preheat oven to 400°
- ◆ Combine all the ingredients in a large bowl.
- ◆ Place 1 Tbls. of the mixture on a phyllo square at one end. Fold the pastry to form a triangle.
- ◆ Bake in oven 10-15 minutes or until browned.

# GREEN BEANS AND TOMATOES

Serves 6

2 Tbls. olive oil
1 small onion, chopped
1½ pounds green beans
3 tomatoes, chopped

¼ cup parsley
¼ cup fresh basil, chopped
Salt, pepper to taste
¼ cup parmesan cheese

- ◆ In a large skillet heat the olive oil. Stir in onion, green beans and tomatoes. Cook for 5 minutes. Stir in parsley and basil. Season with salt and pepper.
- ◆ Serve with parmesan cheese.
- ◆ An alternative to this is to put all the ingredients in a baking dish and top with cheese. Heat oven to 350°. Bake for ½ hour. Serve hot.

# GREEN BEAN CASSEROLE

Serves 6

½ stick butter
¼ cup flour
1 cup half and half
½ cup heavy cream
1½ pounds green beans, snip ends only

½ pound mushrooms, sliced
1 medium leek, sliced
¼ cup fresh parsley, chopped
2 Tbls. dill, snipped
½ cup parmesan cheese
½ cup breadcrumbs

- ◆ Preheat oven to 350°
- ◆ Melt butter in a sauce pan. Stir in flour and half and half until thickened. Stir in cream.
- ◆ In a baking dish combine the green beans, mushrooms, leek, parsley, dill and cream sauce.
- ◆ Pour the parmesan cheese and breadcrumbs on top.
- ◆ Bake 25 minutes, or until bubbling.

# VEGETABLE GRATIN

Serves 6

6 red bliss potatoes
2 medium turnips
1 large leek, sliced
½ stick butter

¼ cup basil, chopped
1 cup heavy cream
1 cup Gruyere cheese, grated

- ◆ Preheat oven to 375°
- ◆ Peel the potatoes and turnips. Thinly slice or use mandolin. Place in large baking dish. Cover with sliced leeks. Dot with butter and basil.
- ◆ Pour cream on top and then grated cheese.
- ◆ Bake for 45 minutes or until vegetables are tender. If not quite browned on top place under broiler for a moment.

# VEGETABLE CASSEROLE

Serves 4

1 small onion, chopped
2 stalks celery, chopped
2 tomatoes, chopped
1 can kidney beans, drained
1 10 oz. package lima beans
½ red bell pepper, chopped

¼ cup parsley, chopped
¼ cup basil, chopped
1 teaspoon pepper
½ teaspoon salt
½ cup cheddar cheese, grated

- ◆ Preheat oven to 350°
- ◆ Combine all the ingredients in a casserole. Top with cheese.
- ◆ Bake ½ hour or until bubbling.


# VEGETABLE STEW

Serves

2 Tbls. olive oil
1 medium onion, sliced
½ red pepper, chopped
½ yellow pepper, chopped
2 carrots, peeled and sliced
1 teaspoon coriander
½ teaspoon cumin
½ teaspoon cinnamon

¼ teaspoon cayenne
4 large tomatoes, chopped
1 15oz. can garbanzo beans
½ cup raisins
¼ cup almonds
Juice of 1 lemon
1 cup couscous
1 cup water

- ◆ Preheat oven to 300°
- ◆ Combine all ingredients in a large covered baking dish.
- ◆ Bake for 1 hour.
- ◆ Chicken broth can be substituted for water.
- ◆ Serve with toasted almonds and feta or mozzarella cheese

# VEGETABLE CASSEROLE

Serves 4

1 small onion, chopped
2 carrots, chopped
4 red bliss potatoes, cubed
½ pound mushrooms, sliced

2 tomatoes, sliced
2 bay leaves
2 cloves garlic, minced
1 cup red wine

- ♦ Preheat oven to 350°
- ♦ Combine the ingredients in a baking dish.
- ♦ Bake ½ hour or until bubbling.

# CURRIED VEGETABLES

Serves 4-6

½ stick butter
2 carrots, sliced
2 red bliss potatoes, diced
½ pound cauliflower, chopped
1 small onion, chopped
2 cloves garlic, minced
¼ cup flour

1½ cups chicken stock
2 Tbls. curry
1 teaspoon cumin
2 tbls. fresh grated ginger
1 teaspoon chili powder
¼ cup cilantro, chopped
Shredded coconut

- ♦ In a skillet melt the butter. Stir in the carrots, potatoes, cauliflower, and onion. Saute for 5 minutes.
- ♦ Stir in garlic and flour. Add stock and thicken.
- ♦ Stir in spices.
- ♦ Serve hot garnished with cilantro and coconut.

# BLUE CHEESE MASHED POTATOES

Serves 6

6 medium red bliss potatoes
½ cup light cream
2 Tbls. butter

½ pound blue cheese, crumbled
2 Tbls. bourbon

- ♦ In a sauce pan boil the potatoes until tender. Place the potatoes in a bowl with rest of the ingredients. Mash until just smooth.
- ♦ Serve warm.
- ♦ Instead of red bliss potatoes, baking potatoes may be substituted. Bake potatoes for 1 hour. Remove from oven. Make a rectangular opening in the top of the potato and remove pulp. Mash the pulp with the rest of the ingredients and restuff potatoes. Place under broiler until just bubbling.

# POTATO CAKES

Serves 6

6 medium potatoes
½ stick butter
½ cup milk
½ cup cream

1 scallion, chopped
Salt and pepper
Flour

- ♦ Cook the potatoes in boiling water until just tender. Drain.
- ♦ Mash with milk, cream, butter and scallions.
- ♦ Make into six patties. Dust with flour.
- ♦ Saute in butter until browned.
- ♦ Serve with herb butter

*Herb Butter*

½ stick butter, softened
1 scallion, chopped
2 chives, chopped

½ cup parsley, chopped
2 cloves garlic, chopped
Juice of ½ lemon

Combine all ingredients in a bowl.

# ROASTED POTATOES

Serves 6

3 red bliss potatoes, cubed
3 medium sweet potatoes, peeled and cubed

¼ cup olive oil
1 Tbls kosher salt
¼ cup rosemary

- ♦ Preheat oven to 375°
- ♦ Place all the ingredients in an iron skillet.
- ♦ Bake for 45 minutes.

# POTATOES WITH PORTABELLAS

Serves 6-8

½ stick butter, melted
6 medium red bliss potatoes, sliced
1 cup leeks, chopped
1 teaspoon salt

1 teaspoon pepper
½ pound portabella mushrooms
2 large tomatoes, sliced
1 cup fresh baby spinach
1 cup cheddar cheese

- ♦ Preheat oven to 350°
- ♦ Pour a small amount of the butter into a baking dish. Line the dish with the potatoes. Sprinkle the leeks with salt and pepper.
- ♦ Put mushrooms, tomatoes and spinach on top of leeks. Sprinkle with rest of butter and cheese.
- ♦ Bake ½ hour or until bubbling.

# STUFFED PORTABELLAS

Serves 6

6 portabella mushroom caps
½ stick butter
½ small onion, chopped
½ pound baby spinach

2 Granny Smith apples, finely chopped
1 Tbls. curry

- ♦ Preheat oven to 350°.
- ♦ Melt the butter in a skillet. Add the onion and sauté until tender. Add the spinach until just wilted. Stir in the apples and curry.
- ♦ Stuff the portabellas with the spinach mixture.
- ♦ Bake 15 minutes.


# BAKED ACORN SQUASH

Serves 6

3 acorn squash, cut in half lengthwise and seeds removed
3 pears or apples, peeled, cored and sliced
Juice of 1 lemon juice
Zest of 1 lemon

3 Tbls. fresh grated ginger
6 Tbls. butter, melted
½ cup honey
1 cup raisins
1 cup walnuts

- ♦ Preheat the oven to 350°
- ♦ In a pressure cooker or large pot cook the squash until just tender. Place on a baking sheet.
- ♦ Combine the rest of the ingredients in a bowl.
- ♦ Fill the squash halves with the mixture.
- ♦ Bake for 12 minutes or until bubbling.
- ♦ ½ cup maple syrup can be substituted for the honey.

# GLAZED CARROTS

Serves 6

1 pound fresh baby carrots
½ pound parsnips, peeled and sliced
¼ cup honey
¼ cup orange juice

Juice of 1 lime
Zest of 1 lime
2 Tbls. fresh grated ginger
½ stick butter

- Combine all the ingredients, except butter in a bowl. Chill overnight.
- Melt the butter in the skillet. Saute carrots and parsnips until just tender. Remove from skillet. Add honey mixture to pan. Bring to a boil and simmer for 5 minutes, or until it starts to thicken. Add carrots and parsnips.
- Serve in a serving bowl.
- Can be garnished with fresh mint.

# BRAISED SPINACH

Serves 4

½ stick butter
2 Tbls. olive oil
1 pound fresh baby spinach

¼ pound country ham, diced
4 cloves garlic, minced

- Melt the butter in a skillet and add the olive oil. Quickly stir in spinach in batches. Stir in ham and garlic.
- Serve immediately.

# BROCCOLI CASSEROLE

Serves 6-8

1 stick butter
½ cup flour
2 cups half and half
½ pound cheddar cheese
½ pound mushrooms, sliced

2 pounds broccoli heads, chopped
1 can sliced water chestnuts
1 cup fine bread crumbs

- ♦ Preheat oven to 350°
- ♦ Melt the butter in a sauce pan. Stir in flour. Add half and half. Stir until thickened. Add cheddar cheese.
- ♦ Place the broccoli, mushrooms and water chestnuts in a greased casserole.
- ♦ Top with sauce and then bread crumbs.
- ♦ Bake ½ hour.
- ♦ Adding 2-3 cups chickens makes for a whole meal.

# BRAISED CABBAGE

Serves 8-10

2 pounds red cabbage, shredded
½ cup vinegar
1 Tbls. sugar
4 apples, peeled, cored and sliced
8 slices bacon

1 medium onion, peeled and sliced
½ cup red wine
2 cups beef bouillon
Salt and pepper to taste

- ♦ In a bowl combine the cabbage, vinegar, sugar, and apples in a bowl. Refrigerate.
- ♦ In a large pot brown the bacon. Remove. Add onions and cook until transparent. Add the cabbage mixture. Stir in the bouillon and wine.
- ♦ Simmer for 45 minutes. Season with salt and pepper.

# SALADS

Jellied Salad

*"What is more refreshing than salads when your appetite seems to have deserted you, or even after a capacious dinner - the nice, fresh, green, and crisp salad, full of life and health, which seems to invigorate the palate and dispose the masticating powers to a much longer duration."*
Alexis Soyer 19th century French chef.

# CRAB SALAD

Serves 4

¼ cup fresh basil, chopped
½ cup mayonnaise
2 Tbls. lemon juice
1 stalk celery, chopped
4 chives, snipped
¼ cup parsley
1 pound crab meat

Red lettuce leaves
2 avocado, sliced in half
1 cucumber, sliced
24 grape tomatoes
4 hard-boiled eggs, cut in half
Fresh basil leaves
Paprika

- ♦ In a bowl combine the basil, mayonnaise, lemon juice, celery, green onion and parsley. Fold in crab.
- ♦ Place the lettuce leaves on each plate. Divide crab mixture into avocado halves on the 4 plates. Surround with cucumber, tomatoes, and hard-boiled eggs.
- ♦ Garnish with basil and paprika.

# CRAB SALAD

Serves 4

Boston lettuce leaves
2 large ripe avocados, cut in half
2 mango, peeled and sliced
Juice of 1 large lemon

1 pound fresh crab meat
Remoulade sauce – p.203
Fresh basil
4 lemon slices

- ◆ Place the lettuce on 4 plates. Top with avocado half. Place the mango around the avocado. Sprinkle the avocado and mango with lemon juice.
- ◆ Divide the crab between the four plates. Top with remoulade sauce.
- ◆ Garnish with basil leaves and lemon slices.
- ◆ Shrimp can be substituted for the crab.

# CRAB SALAD

Serves 4

2 bunches watercress, stems cut off

2 large avocados, cut in half
1 pound crab meat

- ◆ Divide the watercress between the four plates. Place the avocados on top. Divide crab between 4 avocados. Top with lime vinaigrette.

*Lime Vinaigrette*

¼ cup olive oil
¼ cup lime juice
2 cloves garlic, minced
1 Tbls. Dijon mustard

2 green onions, chopped
1 teaspoon sea salt
¼ cup basil
2 Tbls. capers

- ◆ Combine all the ingredients in a bowl.

# OYSTER SALAD

Serves 6

¾ pound baby spinach
24 fried oysters - p
6 slices bacon, cooked and
crumbled

6 hardboiled eggs, sliced
1 large red onion, sliced

♦ Divide the spinach among 6 plates. Garnish the plates with the oysters, bacon, eggs and onion. Top with vinaigrette.

*Creole Honey Mustard Dressing*

¼ cup olive oil
¼ cup lemon juice
¼ cup honey
¼ teaspoon cayenne

1 teaspoon chili powder
½ teaspoon cumin
1 Tbls. fresh grated ginger
1 teaspoon dry mustard

♦ Combine ingredients in a bowl.

# SEAFOOD SALAD

Serves 6

1 ½ pounds crab meat
1½ pounds medium shrimp, cooked, peeled and deveined
1½ pounds thin spring asparagus, blanched and cut in 2 inch pieces

2 cups corn
3 avocados, peeled, pitted and sliced
6 chives, snipped
¾ pound mesclun

♦ In a bowl combine all ingredients. Serve with dill dressing.

*Dill Dressing*

¼ cup lemon juice
¼ cup olive oil

¼ cup dill, snipped
¼ cup basil, chopped

♦ In a bowl combine all ingredients.

# HOT SEAFOOD SALAD

Serves 12

1 pound smoked salmon, cut into pieces
1 pound smoked rockfish fillet, cut into pieces
1 pound medium shrimp, cooked, peeled and deveined
1 pound fresh crab meat

4 large tomatoes, chopped
6 green onions, chopped
2 15 oz cans artichoke hearts, drained
1 pound baby spinach
2 cups walnuts
3 medium cucumbers sliced

- ◆ Combine all the seafood in a bowl. Add vinaigrette, tomatoes, onions, and artichoke hearts.
- ◆ Place the spinach on 12 plates.
- ◆ Top with seafood mixture.
- ◆ Garnish with walnuts and cucumbers.

*Hot Vinaigrette*

¾ cup olive oil
¼ cup balsamic vinegar

½ cup lemon juice

- ◆ In a sauce pan heat the ingredients.


# PEAR SALAD

Serves 4

½ pound mixed spring greens
3 pears, peeled, pitted and sliced

1 cup spiced walnuts
Shaved Asiago cheese

- ◆ Combine the ingredients in a bowl. Toss with Sherry Vinaigrette

*Sherry Vinaigrette*

¼ cup Sherry vinegar or Sherry
¼ cup olive oil

2 Tbls. honey

- ◆ Combine the ingredients in a bowl.

# FIG SALAD

Serves 6

6 large romaine lettuce leaves
1 pound fresh or dried figs
Spiced pecans, p. 32

½ pound Gorgonzola cheese,
crumbled
Balsamic vinaigrette, p.208

- ◆ Place 1 lettuce leaf on each salad plate.
- ◆ Top with figs, pecans and Gorgonzola. Sprinkle some of the vinaigrette over each serving.
- ◆ If preferred all ingredients can be combined in a salad bowl.
- ◆ Pears, apples, or dried apricots can be substituted for the figs.

# AVOCADO SALAD

Serves 6

2 ripe large avocados, peeled,
pitted and sliced
2 apples, peeled, cored and
sliced
2 peaches, peeled, pitted and
sliced

2 kiwi, peeled and sliced
1 mango, peeled and sliced
¼ cup honey
¼ cup fresh lemon juice
¼ cup macadamia nuts
¼ cup coconut

- ◆ Combine all the ingredients in a bowl. Serve immediately or can be served chilled.

# AVOCADO SALAD

Serves 6

6 slices bacon, crumbled
3 avocados, peeled and sliced
2 large tomatoes, sliced
3 green onions, chopped
¼ cup olive oil

2 Tbls. vinegar
¼ cup lemon juice
Salt, pepper
½ pound spring mixed greens
½ pound feta cheese, crumbled

♦ Toss all ingredients in a salad bowl.


# GREEN BEAN SALAD

10 servings

1 pound fresh green beans, ends
sniped
2 large zucchini, sliced
1 small cauliflower, chopped
4 green onion, chopped
20 cherry tomatoes

½ red bell pepper, chopped
20 Greek olives
½ cup olive oil
½ cup lemon
¼ cup fresh oregano
2 large garlic cloves, minced

♦ Toss all ingredients in a salad bowl.

# BEAN SALAD

Serves 10

1 pound green beans, blanched
1 15 oz. can kidney beans, drained
1 pound waxed beans, blanched
1 medium red onion, sliced
1 red bell pepper, sliced
¼ cup olive oil

¼ cup balsamic vinegar
¼ cup fresh lemon juice
Dash Tabasco
1 teaspoon kosher salt
2 teaspoons fresh ground pepper
3 cloves garlic, minced

- ◆ Toss all ingredients in a salad bowl.


# GREEN BEAN SALAD

Serves 4

1 pound green beans, ends snipped
4 slices bacon
1 medium red onion, sliced

½ cup sour cream
2 Tbls. red wine
2 Tbls. dill, snipped

- ◆ Cook the bacon in a skillet. Remove and add onion. Cook until translucent.
- ◆ Blanche the beans for 3 minutes.
- ◆ Combine all ingredients in a salad bowl.

# BEAN AND CORN SALAD

Serves 4

1 15 oz. can black beans
2 cups fresh corn
½ red bell pepper, chopped
¼ cup cilantro, chopped
3 cloves garlic, minced

1 small red onion, chopped
¼ pound Monterrey Jack cheese, grated
¼ cup olive oil
¼ cup lime juice

♦ Toss all ingredients in a bowl.

# CHICKEN SALAD

Serves 4

4 grilled boneless chicken breasts, cubed
1 cup peanuts
2 apples, peeled, cored and chopped
2 stalks celery, chopped
1 Tbls. curry

¼ teaspoon cumin
2 Tbls. fresh grated ginger
½ cup coconut
½ cup sour cream or yogurt
½ cup mayonnaise
2 Tbls. lemon juice
¼ cup cilantro, chopped

♦ Combine all the ingredients in a bowl.
♦ Place on individual plates and garnish with extra coconut and cilantro leaves.
♦ Mint leaves can be substituted for the cilantro.

# CHICKEN SALAD

Serves 4

4 grilled boneless chicken breasts
½ pound dried apricots
1 cup toasted almonds

2 green onions, chopped
¼ cup lime juice
¼ cup olive oil

- ♦ Toss the ingredients in a bowl.
- ♦ Serve on lettuce leaves. Garnish with lime slices.

# GRILLED CHICKEN SALAD

Serves 4

4 boneless grilled chicken breasts, cubed
½ pound Jarlsberg cheese, cut in cubes

½ pound mixed spring greens
½ pound mushrooms, sliced
16 cherry tomatoes
2 green onions, chopped

In a bowl combine all ingredients.
Serve with Stilton blue cheese dressing, p. 207
Sweet Vidalia onion dressing, p. 207
 Or tomato basil vinaigrette, p. 207

# CHICKEN SALAD

Serves 4

4 grilled boneless chicken breasts
2 Tbls. olive oil
2 red bell peppers, sliced
1 large red onion, sliced

2 large tomatoes, sliced
½ pound mushrooms, sliced
1 cup salted cashews
½ pound fresh baby spinach

- ♦ In a skillet warm the olive oil Sauté the red peppers and onions until onions are translucent. Add tomatoes, mushrooms, and cashews.
- ♦ Serve chicken breasts on bed of fresh spinach. Top with vegetables and sesame vinaigrette.

*Sesame Vinaigrette*

¼ cup olive oil
¼ cup lemon juice

¼ cup sesame seeds

- ♦ Combine the ingredients on a bowl.

# CHICKEN SALAD

Serves 4

4 boneless grilled chicken breasts, cubed
2 stalks celery, chopped
1 cup walnuts
1 cup mayonnaise
2 scallions, chopped

4 slices cooked bacon, crumbled
½ pound mushrooms, sliced
1 medium cucumber, sliced
¼ cup parsley
Romaine or Boston lettuce

- ♦ In a bowl combine the chicken celery, walnuts, mayonnaise, and scallions.
- ♦ Put a lettuce leaf on each of 4 plates. Top with chicken mixture.
- ♦ Garnish with bacon, mushrooms, cucumber slices and parsley.

# CURRIED CHICKEN SALAD

Serves 4

4 cups cooked chicken
½ pound green grapes
2 stalks celery, chopped
½ cup mayonnaise
½ cup sour cream
½ cup toasted almonds

2 Tbls. lemon juice
2 green onion, chopped
1 Tbls. curry
2 Tbls. grated fresh ginger
¼ cup coconut

- ♦ Combine the ingredients in a bowl.
- ♦ Serve on lettuce leaves and with chutney.


# CURRIED CHICKEN SALAD II

Serves 4

4 cups cooked chicken
1 large celery stalk, chopped
½ pound seedless grapes
1 cup peanuts
1 Tbls. curry
2 Tbls. fresh grated ginger

½ teaspoon cumin
½ cup mayonnaise
½ cup sour cream
2 tomatoes chopped
½ cup cilantro, chopped

- ♦ Combine all ingredients in a bowl.
- ♦ Serve on lettuce leaves with chutney.

# CHICKEN SALAD

Serves 4

4 grilled chicken breasts
1 15 oz. can black beans
1 red bell pepper, sliced
¼ cup cilantro, chopped
2 tomatoes, chopped
¼ cup olive oil

¼ cup lime juice
2 cloves garlic, minced
1 teaspoon fresh ground pepper
2 avocado, peeled, pitted and sliced
Sour cream

- ◆ Combine all the ingredients, except sour cream, in a bowl.
- ◆ Chill or serve immediately with sour cream and garnish with extra cilantro.

# SOUTHWEST CHICKEN SALAD

Serves 4

4 romaine lettuce leaves
4 boneless grilled chicken breasts, cut in strips
2 large tomatoes, chopped
4 green onions, chopped

2 red bell peppers, sliced
2 jalapenos, seeded and sliced
4 tortillas
Oil

- ◆ Please 1 romaine lettuce leaf on each of 4 plates. Place the chicken slices on top of the lettuce leaves. Top with tomatoes, green onions, and peppers. Top with cilantro vinaigrette.
- ◆ Slice the tortillas into strips. Heat oil in a skillet and quickly fry tortilla strips. Place strips on top of chicken and vegetables.

*Cilantro Vinaigrette*

¼ cup olive oil
¼ cup lime juice
¼ cup cilantro

1 teaspoon kosher salt
1 teaspoon fresh ground pepper

- ◆ Combine all ingredients in a bowl.

# CHICKEN SALAD

Serves 4

4 cups cooked chicken
1 cup celery, diced
1 cup walnuts
½ cup sour cream

½ cup mayonnaise
¼ cup fresh tarragon
Salt and pepper
¼ cup lime or lemon juice

♦ Combine all ingredients in bowl. Serve on bed of mixed greens.

# TURKEY SALAD

This is a good way to use up leftover turkey and rice

Serves 4

4 cups cooked turkey, cubed
½ pound mushrooms, sliced
¼ cup lemon juice
2 cups cooked rice
½ cup mayonnaise
½ cup sour cream
½ red bell pepper, chopped

2 green onion, chopped
¼ cup fresh parsley
1 teaspoon salt
1 teaspoon fresh ground pepper
2 Tbls. basil, chopped
2 Tbls. tarragon, chopped

♦ Combine all the ingredients in a bowl.
♦ Serve on a bed of lettuce. Garnish with lemon slices and basil leaves.
♦ Chicken can be substituted for the turkey
♦ Pasta can be substituted for the rice

# POTATO SALAD

Serves 4

4 medium red bliss potatoes, cooked and cubed
½ small red onion, chopped
1 carrot, peeled and sliced
2 stalks celery, chopped
¼ cup parsley
½ cup mayonnaise
½ cup sour cream

2 Tbls. tarragon vinegar
2 Tbls. dill weed
1 teaspoon kosher salt
1 teaspoon pepper
4 slices bacon, cooked and crumbled
¼ pound blue cheese, crumbled

- ♦ Combine all ingredients, except bacon and blue cheese in a bowl.
- ♦ Garnish with bacon and cheese.
- ♦ Can also be served on a platter on a bed of lettuce.

# POTATO SALAD

Serves 6-8

8 red bliss potatoes, cubed and boiled till tender
1 cup mayonnaise
½ cup sour cream
8 slices bacon, cooked and crumbled
4 green onions
¼ cup parsley
1 teaspoon salt
1 teaspoon pepper

1 teaspoon celery seed
1 cup grated cheddar cheese
4 stalks celery
2 red bell pepper, chopped
8 hardboiled eggs, cut in half
15 cherry tomatoes
Lettuce leaves
Paprika
Fresh basil

- ♦ Combine all ingredients in a bowl, except eggs, cherry tomatoes, lettuce, basil and paprika.
- ♦ Place the lettuce leaves on a platter. Spoon the salad mixture on leaves. Garnish with eggs, tomatoes, paprika and basil.

# DILLED POTATO SALAD

Serves 6

6 medium red bliss potatoes
½ cup red onion, chopped
¼ cup sour cream

¼ cup mayonnaise
¼ cup fresh dill, snipped
Salt and pepper to taste

- ◆ Cube potatoes, leaving skins on and boil until tender. Cool in a bowl.
- ◆ Toss with remaining ingredients.
- ◆ Serve on a bed of lettuce and garnish with tomato wedges, cucumber slices and quartered hard-boiled eggs. Sprinkle with paprika.

# WATERCRESS POTATO SALAD

Serves 6

6 large red bliss potatoes
2 bunches watercress
1 pint cherry tomatoes
2 Tbls. red wine vinegar

2 Tbls. olive oil
2 Tbls. lemon juice
2 Tbls. fresh basil, chopped

- ◆ Boil the potatoes in a pan until tender. Cool. Slice thinly.
- ◆ In a salad bowl combine the vinegar, olive oil, lemon juice and basil.
- ◆ Toss in the potatoes, watercress and tomatoes.
- ◆ Serve chilled
- ◆ For a hearty meal, grilled chicken or beef can be added to the salad.

# WATERCRESS SALAD

Serves 4

2 bunches watercress
1 cup candied walnuts - p
1 cup blue cheese
4 Clementine oranges, peeled
and sectioned

Juice of 2 Clementines
Zest of Clementines
¼ cup honey

♦ Toss all ingredients in a salad bowl.


# FRUIT SALAD

Serves 4

2 avocados, peeled pitted and
sliced
2 stalks celery, sliced
2 apples, peeled, cored and
sliced

2 bananas, peeled and sliced
½ cup raisins
½ cup walnuts

♦ Toss the ingredients in a bowl with the dressing.

*Honey Dressing*

2 Tbls olive oil
¼ cup lemon or lime juice

¼ cup honey
Zest of 1 lemon or lime

♦ Combine the ingredients in a bowl.

# FRUIT SALAD

Serves 6-8

1 large mango, peeled and sliced
2 bananas, peeled and sliced
1 pineapple, skinned, cored and sliced
2 peaches, peeled, pitted and sliced

2 kiwi, peeled and sliced
½ cup sour cream
Juice of 1 lime
½ cup toasted almonds
¼ cup toasted coconut

♦ Combine all ingredients in a bowl, except almonds and coconut.
♦ Garnish with almonds and coconut.
♦ Yogurt can be substituted for sour cream

# ORANGE AND GRAPEFRUIT SALAD

Serves 4

3 oranges, peeled and sectioned, removing all white and saving juice
2 grapefruit, peeled and sectioned and saving juice

¼ cup balsamic vinegar
1 Tbls. sugar
2 bunches watercress

♦ Toss all ingredients in a salad bowl.
♦ Sliced avocado can also be added.

# STRAWBERRY SALAD

Serves 6

2 grapefruit, peeled and sectioned, save juice
2 avocado, peeled, pitted and sliced
1 quart strawberries
½ pound spring greens

¼ cup lemon juice
¼ cup orange juice
2 Tbls.sugar
¼ cup heavy cream
2 Tbls. balsamic vinegar

- ♦ Toss all the ingredients in a bowl.

# BROCCOLI SALAD

Serves 4

1 pound broccoli florets
2 green onions, chopped
12 Greek pitted olives
¼ cup mayonnaise
¼ cup sour cream

2 Tbls. vinegar
12 grape tomatoes
4 hardboiled eggs
1 Tbls. oregano

- ♦ Combine all ingredients in bowl, except tomatoes, eggs and oregano.
- ♦ Garnish with tomatoes, eggs and oregano.

# BROCCOLI SALAD

Serves 4-6

1 pound broccoli florets
2 large avocados, peeled, pitted and sliced
2 Tbls lemon juice
2 Tbls. Dijon mustard

2 cloves garlic, minced
2 Tbls. Balsamic vinegar
2 Tbls. olive oil
Salt and pepper to taste

- ♦ Combine the ingredients in a salad bowl.

# TOMATO ASPIC

Serves 6

4 cups V8 juice
2 green onions, chopped
1 teaspoon fresh ground pepper
2 Tbls. fresh basil, chopped
2 envelopes gelatin
¼ cup dry white wine

Juice of 1 lemon
2 avocados, peeled, pitted and diced
½ yellow pepper, chopped
½ red bell pepper, chopped

- ♦ In a sauce pan combine the V8 juice, green onion, pepper and basil. Bring to a boil. Remove from heat.
- ♦ In a cup stir the gelatin into the wine. Pour into the pan and stir until dissolved. Stir in the lemon juice.
- ♦ Arrange the avocados and peppers in a 1½ quart mold. Pour V8 mixture into mold.
- ♦ Chill for at least 4 hours, or until set.
- ♦ Serve with sour cream, chives, or sliced green onions.

# SLICED TOMATOES

6 large ripe tomatoes, sliced
1 teaspoon kosher salt
1 teaspoon fresh ground pepper
1 Tbls. thyme
1 Tb.s marjoram

¼ cup parsley, chopped
¼ cup fresh basil, chopped
4 chives, snipped
¼ cup olive oil
¼ cup vinegar

In a bowl combine all ingredients. Refrigerate for at least four hours.

# TOMATO AND BRIE SALAD

Serves 6

4 large tomatoes, sliced
1 round herb crusted brie, sliced
½ cup toasted pine nuts

½ pound mixed spring greens
2 Tbls. balsamic vinegar
¼ cup olive oil

♦ Combine all ingredients in a salad bowl.

# SPINACH SALAD

I came up with this idea one winter when we had no fresh fruit in the house and had run out of honey

Serves 4

½ pound baby spinach
½ pound dried apricots
1 cup macadamia nuts
¼ pound blue cheese, crumbled

¼ cup lemon juice
¼ cup maple syrup

♦ Toss all ingredients in a salad bowl.

# SPINACH SALAD

Serves 4

½ pound baby spinach
2 apples, cored and sliced
1 cup macadamia nuts

1 cup raisins
¼ cup maple syrup
¼ cup lemon juice

♦ Toss all ingredients in a salad bowl.

# SPINACH SALAD

Serves 4

4 slices bacon
½ pound sun-dried tomatoes, chopped
2 Tbls. balsamic vinegar

½ pound baby spinach
1 cup candied pecans - p
12 cherry tomatoes
1 can fried onion rings

♦ Fry the bacon in a skillet until crisp. Remove bacon and crumble. Add sun-dried tomatoes and vinegar to skillet. Stir until tomatoes are just tender.
♦ In a bowl toss the spinach with the pecans, bacon, tomatoes and sun-dried tomato mixture. Garnish with fried onion rings.

# BABY SPINACH SALAD

Serves 4

4 roasted red peppers, sliced
1 small red onion, sliced
½ pound shitaki mushrooms
½ pound baby spinach

6 slices bacon, cooked and bacon fat reserved
2 hardboiled eggs, sliced

♦ Toss all the ingredients in a salad bowl with vinaigrette.

*Warm Bacon Vinaigrette*

Bacon fat
¼ cup vinegar

¼ cup honey

♦ Using the skillet the bacon was cooked in add fat, vinegar and honey.

# ORANGE SPINACH SALAD

Serves 4

½ pound baby spinach
2 oranges, peeled and sliced
1 cup pecans
1 cup Gorgonzola cheese, crumbled

¼ cup orange juice
2 Tbls. olive oil
2 Tbls. honey

♦ Toss the ingredients in a salad bowl.


# SPINACH SALAD WITH PEARS

Serves 4

½ pound baby spinach
2 pears, peeled, cored and sliced
½ cup curried almonds

4 slices smoked bacon, cooked and crumbled
¼ cup lemon juice
¼ cup honey

♦ Toss all the ingredients in a salad bowl.


# ROASTED BEET SALAD

Serves 6

6 large beets
1 cup blue cheese, crumbled
1 cup walnuts
½ pound baby spinach

¼ cup orange juice
2 Tbls. lemon juice
¼ cup honey
1 teaspoon salt

♦ Heat oven to 400°
♦ Place the beets on a cookie sheet and bake for ½ hour, or until tender.
♦ Remove beet skins. Slice beets.
♦ In a salad bowl toss all ingredients.

# VEGETABLE SALAD

Serves 8-10

2 large tomatoes, sliced
1 medium cucumber, sliced
1 red pepper, cut into strips
1 yellow pepper, cut into strips
6 red bliss potatoes, cooked, and
quartered
½ medium red onion, sliced
2 celery stalks

½ pound blue or feta cheese,
crumbled
½ pound baby spinach
12 Kalamata olives
¼ cup olive oil
¼ cup fresh lemon juice
¼ cup honey
Salt and pepper to taste

♦ Combine all the ingredients in a large salad bowl.

# GARDEN SALAD

Serves 4

½ pound spring greens
1 medium cucumber, sliced
12 grape tomatoes
2 scallion, sliced

1 teaspoon fresh ground pepper
¼ cup mayonnaise
½ cup heavy cream
¼ pound crumbled blue cheese

♦ In bowl combine the spring greens, cucumber, tomatoes and scallion.
♦ In a separate bowl beat the whipped cream. Fold in the mayonnaise, pepper and blue cheese. Serve over the salad.

# DILLED CUCUMBERS

Serves 6-8

2 medium cucumbers
2 teaspoons sea salt
¼ cup vinegar
1 Tbls. sugar

½ teaspoon paprika
3 green onions, chopped
¼ cup fresh dill

- ◆ Combine all ingredients in a bowl.
- ◆ Serve chilled.


# CUCUMBERS IN SOUR CREAM

Serves

2 medium cucumber, sliced
1 teaspoon kosher salt
1 Tbls. sugar
¼ cup cider vinegar
1 ½ cups sour cream

2 Tbls. dill, snipped
2 Tbls. chives, snipped
3 green onions, chopped
1 teaspoon celery salt

- ◆ Combine all ingredients in a bowl. Serve chilled.


# CUCUMBER TOMATO SALAD

Serves 6

2 medium cucumbers, sliced
3 large ripe tomatoes, sliced
3 green onions, chopped
3 Tbls. fresh dill, chopped

¼ cup Balsamic vinegar
¼ cup olive oil
½ teaspoon cumin
Salt, pepper to taste

- ◆ Toss the ingredients in a salad bowl.
- ◆ Red onion can be substituted for the green onions.

# PASTAS AND RICE

The author's mother Kay Barney at a picnic

*"Those who forget the pasta are condemned to reheat it."*
Unknown Author

Thomas Jefferson was known to have acquired a pasta machine 1787.

# CRAB IN WHITE WINE SAUCE

Serves 4

1 pound bow-tie pasta
2 Tbls. butter
½ pound portabella mushrooms,
sliced

2 large tomatoes, chopped
1 pound crab meat
White wine sauce, p. 208
Grated parmesan cheese

- ♦ Cook pasta in a sauce pan according to instructions. Drain and put in bowl.
- ♦ Using same pan melt butter and stir in mushrooms and tomatoes. Cook for 3 minutes.
- ♦ Add crab, mushrooms and tomatoes to pasta. Pour white sauce over top. Sprinkle parmesan cheese over sauce.
- ♦ Serve immediately.

# CRAB PASTA

Serves 4

1 pound tricolor pasta
1 pound broccoli florets
12 cherry tomatoes
2 green onions
1 pound crab meat

¼ cup lemon juice
2 Tbs. olive oil
¼ cup fresh basil
Salt and pepper to taste

- ♦ Cook pasta according to directions. Drain.
- ♦ In a bowl combine all ingredients.

# CRAB PASTA

Serves 6

½ pound baby spinach
2 green onion, chopped
1½ pounds penne
¼ cup olive oil
¼ cup lemon juice
¼ cup basil, chopped

1 pound crab meat
1 pound medium shrimp, cooked, peeled and deveined
6 hardboiled eggs, sliced in half
12 black pitted olives
Basil leaves

♦ Cook pasta according to directions. Drain.
♦ In a bowl combine the spinach, green onion, penne, olive oil, lemon juice and basil. Gently fold in the crab and shrimp.
♦ Garnish with the eggs, olives and basil leaves.


# WILD MUSHROOM PASTA

Serves 4

1 pound fettuccine
½ stick butter
½ pound assorted wild mushrooms (chanterelle, oyster or shitaki)
2 tomatoes, chopped
1 small leek, chopped

1 teaspoon sage
1 cup cream
¼ pound prosciutto, cut small pieces
Salt and pepper
Grated Asiago cheese

♦ Cook pasta in a sauce pan according to instructions. Drain.
♦ Melt the butter in the sauce pan. Add mushrooms, tomatoes and leeks. Cook 3 minutes.
♦ Add sage, cream and prosciutto.
♦ Serve in bowl with cheese.

# RISOTTO WITH CHICKEN

Serves 4

2 Tbls. butter
1 cup leeks, chopped
1 red pepper, chopped
½ pound asparagus, cut in 2 inch
pieces

1 ½ cups Arborio rice
3 cups chicken stock
4 cups grilled chicken
Salt and fresh pepper to taste
1 cup grated parmesan cheese

- ◆ In a sauce pan melt the butter. Add the leeks, pepper and asparagus. Stir in rice. Slowly add the stock. Stir for 20-30 minutes until all liquid is absorbed. Add chicken.
- ◆ Serve with grated cheese.

# ASPARAGUS RISOTTO

Serves 8

3 cups chicken broth
2 Tbls. butter
2 green onions, chopped
8 asparagus, sliced
3 cloves garlic, minced
2 cups arborio rice

½ cup dry white wine
1 Tbls. dill
Couple of drops of truffle oil
Salt and pepper to taste
1 cup parmesan cheese, grated

- ◆ In a sauce pan melt the butter. Add onion and asparagus. Stir in rice. Slowly add the stock. Stir for 20-30 minutes until all liquid is absorbed. Add wine, dill, truffle oil, salt and pepper.
- ◆ Serve with grated cheese

# CHICKEN FIORENTINA

Serves 4

1 pound orzo
½ pound baby spinach
4 grilled boneless chicken breasts
½ pound sun-dried tomatoes
¼ cup capers

¼ cup pine nuts
12 black or Greek pitted olives
½ recipe roasted lemon garlic vinaigrette - p
Grated parmesan cheese

- ♦ Cook orzo according to directions. Drain.
- ♦ Place baby spinach on four plates. Top with chicken, then tomatoes, capers, nuts and olives. Sprinkle some of the vinaigrette on top and then grated cheese.

# CHICKEN PORTABELLA

Serves 4

1 pound orzo
½ pound baby spinach
4 grilled boneless chicken breasts

½ pound portabella mushrooms, sliced and grilled
¼ pound smoked mozzarella, sliced

- ♦ Cook orzo according to directions. Drain.
- ♦ Place the orzo on a platter. Top with spinach, chicken, and mushrooms.
- ♦ Drizzle the green sauce over chicken. Top with mozzarella slice.

*Green Sauce*

2 Tbls. shallots, chopped
2 cloves garlic, minced
2 Tbls. capers
¼ cup parsley, finely chopped

¼ cup olive oil
2 Tbls. lemon juice
Salt and pepper

In a bowl combine the ingredients.

# PASTA MILANO

Serves 4

1 pound bowtie pasta
4 chicken breasts, grilled
½ pound sun-dried tomatoes
½ pound mushrooms

Roasted garlic cream – use
white sauce p. 208 and add 3
cloves minced garlic

- ♦ Cook pasta according to instructions. Drain.
- ♦ Serve the pasta in a pasta bowl topped with chicken breasts, tomatoes, mushrooms, and roasted garlic cream sauce.

# CHICKEN WITH VODKA SAUCE

Serves 6

½ stick butter
6 boneless chicken breasts
½ pound prosciutto, sliced
½ pound porcini mushrooms,
sliced

1 pound baby spinach
3 cloves garlic, minced
1 cup heavy cream
½ cup vodka
1 pound penne

- ♦ Cook the penne according to instructions. Put in a large serving bowl or soup tureen.
- ♦ In a large skillet melt the butter and sauté the chicken until browned on each side. Remove the chicken from the skillet and place in bowl with pasta.
- ♦ In the skillet saute the mushrooms, spinach and garlic until just tender. Remove the vegetables. Add the cream to the skillet and then the vodka.
- ♦ Top the chicken with prosciutto, then the spinach mushroom mixture. Pour the cream and vodka over the mixture.
- ♦ Serve warm with crusty bread and a green salad.

# SHRIMP WITH TOMATO CREAM SAUCE

Serves 4

1 pound fettuccine
½ stick butter
2 green onions
3 cloves garlic, minced
2 large tomatoes, chopped

¼ cup basil, chopped
1 cup cream
1 pound shrimp, cooked, peeled and deveined
1 cup Asiago cheese, grated

- ♦ Cook pasta according to directions. Drain
- ♦ In a sauce pan melt the butter. Stir in onions, garlic, tomato and basil. Cook 3 minutes. Stir in cream. Add shrimp.
- ♦ Place the fettuccine in a large pasta bowl. Add shrimp mixture and toss. Serve with grated cheese.

# SHRIMP AND CHICKEN WITH PENNE

Serves 4

1 pound penne
1 pound shrimp cooked, peeled and deveined
2 grilled boneless chicken breasts, cubed

¼ pound prosciutto
¼ cup basil, chopped
Cream sauce – p. 206
1 cup parmesan cheese

- ♦ Cook penne according to directions. Drain.
- ♦ In a pasta bowl combine the ingredients. Sprinkle cheese on top.

# TOMATO BASIL SAUCE WITH SAUSAGE

Serves 4

¼ cup olive oil
1 large onion, sliced
½ red bell pepper, sliced
½ yellow pepper, sliced
3 cloves garlic, minced
4 large tomatoes, chopped
¼ cup basil, chopped

2 teaspoons oregano
1 teaspoon pepper
1 teaspoon salt
1 pound hot Italian sausage
½ cup red wine
1 pound rigatoni
Grated parmesan cheese

- Heat the oven to 400°
- Place the sausage in a baking dish with a small amount of water. Bake until just browned, about 20 minutes. Remove and slice.
- Heat the olive oil in a sauce pan. Add onion and peppers. Cook until onion is transparent. Add garlic, tomatoes, basil, oregano, pepper and salt. Add sausage and wine.
- Cook the rigatoni according to instructions. Drain.
- Put the rigatoni in pasta bowls. Cover with sausage mixture and top with grated cheese.
- The sausage can also be braised in a skillet.
- Other types of sausage can be used such as chicken varieties or other pork sausage.

# PASTA SALAD

Serves 4

1 pound penne, cooked according to directions
1 pound smoked turkey, chopped
16 Greek pitted olives
4 green onion, chopped

1 medium cucumber, sliced
16 grape tomatoes
¼ pound Feta cheese
Cilantro Vinaigrette, use lemon vinaigrette, p. 208 and add
¼ cup cilantro, chopped

- Combine all ingredients in a bowl.

# PASTA SALAD

Serves 6-8

1 pound penne
½ pound feta cheese
15 ounce can artichoke hearts
1 large cucumber, sliced
1 medium red onion, sliced
2 large tomatoes, chopped

¼ cup balsamic vinegar
¼ cup olive oil
¼ cup fresh basil
1 teaspoon kosher salt
1 teaspoon fresh ground pepper

- ♦ Cook the penne according to directions. Drain and put in a bowl.
- ♦ Add the other ingredients. Toss.


# RICE WITH VEGETABLES

Serves 6-8

2 cups basmati rice
1 stick butter
1 large onion, chopped
½ pound green beans, trimmed and cut into 2" lengths
2 large carrots, peeled and sliced

½ medium red pepper, chopped
½ medium green pepper, chopped
1 cup fresh green peas, shelled
¼ cup fresh cilantro
Salt and pepper

- ♦ In a sauce pan boil 4 cups water and add rice. Bring to a boil and reduce heat. Cook for about 15 minutes or until rice is tender.
- ♦ In another pan heat the butter and stir in the onion, green beans, carrots, peppers and peas. Cook until al dente, just tender. Stir in rice and cilantro. Add salt and pepper to taste.
- ♦ Mint can be substituted for the cilantro.

# CURRIED RICE SALAD

Serves 4-6

4 cups cooked chicken, cubed
2 cups cooked rice
1 cup fresh peas
½ pound broccoli florets
1 stalk celery, chopped
2 green onions, chopped
2 Tbls. lemon juice
1 cup mayonnaise
3 cloves garlic, minced

½ teaspoon cumin
1 Tbls. curry
1 Tbls. fresh grated ginger
1 teaspoon chili powder
½ pound baby spinach
½ cup coconut
½ cup peanuts
4 hardboiled eggs, halved
¼ cup cilantro

- In a bowl combine the chicken, rice, peas, broccoli, celery, onions, lemon juice, mayonnaise, and spices.
- Place the spinach leaves on a platter. Spoon the chicken onto the platter.
- Garnish with the coconut, peanuts, eggs and cilantro.

# CURRIED RICE

Serves 4

2 cups basmati rice
3 cups water
½ stick butter
1 small onion, chopped
2 cloves garlic, grated
2 medium apples, peeled, cored
and chopped
1 cup peas

¼ cup flour
2 cups chicken stock
1 Tbls. curry powder
1 Tbls. grated ginger
½ teaspoon cumin
¼ cup cilantro
½ cup coconut

- In a sauce pan bring the water to a boil. Add rice. Bring to boil. Cover and turn off heat. Let sit 15 minutes.
- In a skillet melt the butter and stir in onion. Saute until translucent. Add garlic, apple and peas.
- Stir in flour and stick until slightly thickened. Add spices. Stir in rice and cilantro.
- Serve in bowl garnished with extra cilantro and coconut.

# BLACK BEANS AND RICE

Serves 4

2 cups water
1 cup rice
2 Tbls. olive oil
½ cup green pepper, chopped
2 green onions, chopped
2 jalapeno, seeded and chopped
4 slices cooked bacon, chopped

1 15 oz. can black beans, drained
1 teaspoon oregano
½ teaspoon cumin
¼ teaspoon cayenne
Salt, pepper to taste

- Bring the water to a boil. Add rice. Bring to boil. Cover. Turn off heat and let sit 15 minutes.
- In a separate pan heat olive oil and add peppers and onions. Cook until onions are translucent.
- Add rest of ingredients.
- Serve hot garnished with green onion and cilantro.

# BASMATI RICE

Serves 4

3 cups water
2 cup basmati rice
2 Tbls. olive oil
½ red pepper, chopped
½ yellow pepper, chopped

2 scallions, chopped
2 cloves garlic, minced
1 teaspoon pepper
¼ cup cilantro

- Bring the water to a boil. Add rice. Bring to boil. Cover. Turn off heat and let sit 15 minutes.
- In a separate pan heat olive oil and add peppers and onions. Cook until onions are translucent.
- Add garlic and pepper.
- Serve in bowl garnished with cilantro.

# COUSCOUS WITH MINT AND TOMATOES

This is good with lamb

Serves 6

2 cups couscous
2½ cups water
Juice of 1 lemon

2 medium tomatoes, chopped
¼ cup fresh mint leaves
Salt and pepper

♦ In a sauce pan bring the water to a bowl and add the couscous. Remove from heat and let stand 5 minutes.
♦ Place in a bowl.
♦ Combine the other ingredients with the couscous.
♦ Serve hot or chilled.


# COUSCOUS WITH CURRANTS

Serves 6-8

4 cups chicken broth
½ stick butter
3 cups couscous
1 cup currants

½ cup pine nuts
2 scallions, sliced
¼ cup fresh mint

♦ Bring the broth and butter to a boil in a sauce pan. Remove from heat. Stir in couscous. Cover.
♦ After 5 minutes fluff the couscous. Add the remaining ingredients.
♦ Long grain rice, basmati rice or wild rice can be substituted for the couscous.
♦ Cranberries can be substituted for the currants, and chopped walnuts for the pine nuts.
♦ This can be served hot or chilled.

# BREADS

Oyster Baskets

# HERB BISCUITS

Makes 10-12 biscuits

2 cups flour
1 stick butter
1 Tbls. baking powder
¼ teaspoon salt
¾ cup half and half

2 Tbls. fresh parsley
2 Tbls. fresh basil
½ teaspoon thyme
½ teaspoon marjoram

- ◆ Preheat oven to 400°
- ◆ Combine all the ingredients in a food processor.
- ◆ Roll out on floured surface. Cut with medium size biscuit cutter.
- ◆ Place on ungreased baking sheet.
- ◆ Bake 12 minutes or until browned.
- ◆ Serve with butter, or herb butter.


# APPLE BISCUITS

Makes 12

6 Tbls. butter
2 cups flour
¾ cup half and half

¼ cup sugar
1 cup cheddar cheese

- ◆ Preheat oven to 400°
- ◆ Place all ingredients in food processor until ball forms. Remove dough and place on floured board. Roll out on board.
- ◆ Using a large biscuit cutter cut out biscuits. Place apple slice on each biscuit. Top with cinnamon mixture.
- ◆ Place on cookie sheet. Bake for 12 minutes or until just browned.

*Topping*

2 apples, peeled, cored and sliced
¼ cup brown sugar

¼ cup sugar
1 teaspoon cinnamon

- ◆ Combine brown sugar, sugar and cinnamon in a bowl.

172

# POLENTA

Polenta is one of the easiest cornmeal dishes to make. We like to serve this with grilled salmon and some chopped Greek olives and a little olive oil.

Serves 4

1 cup cornmeal
4 cups water

2 Tbls. butter
½ cup parmesan cheese

- ◆ Preheat oven to 350°
- ◆ Bring water to boil in sauce pan. Add cornmeal. Stir until thickened. Stir in butter and cheese.
- ◆ Pour into greased square baking dish.
- ◆ Bake 15-20 minutes, just browned. Cut in slices.

# CORN FRITTERS

4 cups fresh corn
1 cup flour
2 eggs
½ cup milk

2 teaspoons baking powder
2 jalapeno, chopped
½ cup cheddar cheese, grated
Oil

- ◆ Combine all the ingredients, except oil, in a bowl.
- ◆ Heat the oil in a skillet.
- ◆ Make the dough into balls.
- ◆ Fry in hot oil until browned.
- ◆ Serve with maple syrup.

# SPOONBREAD

1 stick butter
3 cups water
2 cups cornmeal
¼ cup sugar

1 teaspoon salt
3 eggs, beaten
1½ cups milk

- ◆ Preheat oven to 350°.
- ◆ In a sauce pan heat butter and water to a boil. Add cornmeal. Cool. Add other ingredients.
- ◆ Pour into a buttered casserole.
- ◆ Bake 1 hour or until browned.
- ◆ Serve with butter.

# CURRANT SCONES

½ stick butter
1¾ cups flour
¼ cup sugar
2 teaspoons baking powder

1 egg, beaten
½ cup currants
½ cup half and half

- ◆ Preheat oven to 400°
- ◆ Combine all ingredients in bowl. Place dough on floured board. Knead at least a dozen times. Roll ½ inch thick. Cut dough large biscuit cutter.
- ◆ Place on ungreased cookie sheet. Brush with 1 beaten egg.
- ◆ Bake 10-12 or until just golden.
- ◆ Serve with whipped cream, jams or clotted cream.

# BANANA BREAD

1 stick butter
1 cup sugar
1½ cups flour
2 teaspoons baking powder
2 eggs

1 cup bran
3 large bananas, mashed
2 Tbls. lemon juice
1 cup raisins
1 cup walnuts

- ◆ Preheat oven to 350°
- ◆ In a bowl cream the butter and sugar. Beat in the other ingredients.
- ◆ Pour into greased loaf pan. Bake 50-60 minutes, or until toothpick comes out clean.

# SWEET POTATO BREAD

Makes 1 loaf

2 cups flour
1½ cups sugar
1 teaspoon baking soda
½ teaspoon salt
1 cup mashed sweet potatoes
1 teaspoon cinnamon
½ teaspoon nutmeg

1 teaspoon allspice
½ teaspoon ground cloves
½ teaspoon ginger
½ cup chopped dates
½ cup pecans
1 apple, peeled, cored and diced
2 eggs

- ◆ Preheat oven to 350°.
- ◆ Combine the ingredients in a bowl and pour into a greased loaf pan.
- ◆ Bake 1 hour.
- ◆ This is good served with cream cheese.

# APPLE BREAD

Makes 1 loaf

1 egg
1 cup applesauce
½ stick butter
½ cup sugar
½ cup brown sugar
2 ½ cups flour
2 teaspoons baking powder

1 teaspoon cinnamon
½ teaspoon nutmeg
½ teaspoon cloves
½ teaspoon ginger
½ cup raisins
½ cup pecans or walnuts

- ◆ Preheat oven to 350°.
- ◆ In a bowl combine the egg, applesauce, butter and sugars. Stir in the rest of the ingredients.
- ◆ Butter a bread loaf pan. Pour the batter into the loaf pan.
- ◆ Bake for 1 hour or until a toothpick comes out clean. Cool.
- ◆ Serve with cream cheese.

# BUTTER PECAN BREAD

2 ¼ cups flour
2 teaspoons baking powder
½ teaspoon salt
1 teaspoon cinnamon
¼ teaspoon nutmeg
½ cup sugar

½ cup brown sugar
½ teaspoon vanilla
1 cup pecans
1 egg
1 cup milk
1 stick butter

- ◆ Preheat oven to 350°
- ◆ Combine all ingredients in a bowl
- ◆ Pour into 2 greased loaf pans
- ◆ Bake for 45 minutes

# BREAKFAST AND BRUNCH DISHES

What better way to start off Sunday brunch than to have champagne
and fresh oysters

# CRAB OMELET

Serves 4

8 eggs
4 Tbls. butter
1 pound crab meat
4 asparagus, sliced

½ red pepper, diced
1 cup sharp cheddar cheese, grated

- ◆ Preheat oven to 350°
- ◆ Beat the eggs in a large bowl
- ◆ Heat the butter in a large iron skillet. Pour in the eggs. Heat until just bubbling.
- ◆ Add crab meat, asparagus, pepper, and cheese.
- ◆ Put in oven for 15-20 minutes until eggs are set.
- ◆ Slice into 4 quarters and serve on warm plates.

# CRAB OMELET

Serves 4

8 eggs
½ stick butter
1 large tomato, chopped

1 large avocado, peeled, pitted and chopped
1 pound fresh crab meat
¼ cup fresh basil

- ◆ Beat the eggs in a bowl. Heat the butter in a large skillet. Add eggs. Use spatula to keep sides from sticking.
- ◆ When just about cooked, add tomato, avocado, crab and basil on ½ of omelet. Turn off heat and let sit for several minutes.
- ◆ Gently slide omelet out of pan and fold in half.
- ◆ Serve garnished with extra basil.

# CRAB OMELET

Serves 4

½ stick butter
8 eggs
1 cup Gruyere, grated
2 green onions, chopped

½ cup red pepper
1 pound crab meat
Parsley
Lemon slices

- Beat the eggs in a bowl. Heat the butter in a large skillet. Add eggs. Use spatula to keep sides from sticking.
- When just about cooked, add Gruyere, onions, pepper and crab on ½ of omelet. Turn off heat and let sit for several minutes.
- Gently slide omelet out of pan and fold in half.
- Serve garnished with parsley and lemon slices.

# CRAB FRITTATA

Serves 4

½ stick butter
8 eggs
¼ pound baby spinach
2 green onions, chopped
½ cup leek, chopped

2 cooked red bliss potatoes, sliced
1 pound crabmeat
Parsley
Lemon slices

- Preheat oven to 400°
- Beat the eggs in a bowl. Heat the butter in a large skillet. Add eggs. Use spatula to keep sides from sticking.
- When about half cooked, add spinach, onions, leeks, potatoes and crab.
- Place in onion for 15 minutes or until just lightly browned.
- Serve garnished with parsley and lemon slices.

# CRAB OMELET WITH NEWBURG SAUCE

Serves 4

½ stick butter  
8 eggs  
1 pound crab meat  

Paprika  
Parsley  

- ◆ Melt the butter in a skillet.
- ◆ Beat the eggs in a bowl. Pour into skillet. Use spatula to keep sides from sticking. Cook until firm.
- ◆ Place crab meat on ½ of the omelet. Gently slide omelet out of pan and fold in half. Cut in four pieces and serve with Newburg sauce.
- ◆ Garnish with paprika and parsley.

*Newburg Sauce*

½ stick butter  
¼ cup flour  
1 ½ cups half and half  
3 egg yolks, beaten  

½ pound lobster meat  
¼ cup white wine  
3 Tbls. lemon juice  

- ◆ Melt the butter in a sauce pan. Add flour and slowly stir in flour until thickened. Slowly pour in egg yolks. Stir in lobster, wine and lemon juice.

# CRAB OMELET

Serves 4

½ stick butter  
8 eggs, beaten  
1 large avocado, peeled, pitted and diced  

¼ cup fresh chives, chopped  
½ cup Provolone cheese, shredded  

- ◆ Melt butter in a skillet. Pour in eggs. Use spatula to keep sides from sticking. When almost finished cooking, place avocado, chive, and cheese on ½ omelet.
- ◆ Gently slide omelet out of pan and fold in half.

# CRAB DUMPLINGS

Serves 4

2 eggs, beaten
1 cup milk
2 Tbls. lemon juice
1 teaspoon Worcestershire sauce
Salt and pepper, to taste
1½ teaspoons baking powder
1 cup flour

1 pound crab meat
¼ cup parsley, chopped
2 Tbls. olive oil
2 Tbls. butter
Lemon slices
Parsley

- In a bowl combine the eggs, milk, lemon juice, Worcestershire, salt, pepper, baking powder and flour. Fold in crab and parsley. Shape in to balls.
- Melt the butter and heat olive oil in skillet. Place the crab balls in skillet. Brown on all sides. Add more butter if necessary.
- Garnish with parsley and lemon slices.

# CRABBY MUFFINS

Serves 4

½ stick butter
¼ cup flour
1 ½ cups half and half
½ pound portabella mushrooms, sliced
2 Tbls. tarragon, chopped
2 Tbls. Sherry

1 pound fresh spring asparagus, cut in 2 inch pieces
2 Tbls. lemon juice
1 pound crab meat
Toasted English muffin halves
Parsley
Lemon slices

- Melt the butter in a sauce pan. Add flour, half and half, stirring until thickened. Add mushrooms, tarragon, Sherry, asparagus, and lemon juice.
- Place two muffin halves on each plate. Top with crab meat and sauce. Garnish with parsley and lemon slices.

# CRAB CREPES

Serves 10, 2 crepes each

2 sticks butter
1 cup flour
4 cups half and half
½ cup Sherry
½ stick butter

1 pound mushrooms, sliced
1 pound baby spinach
½ cup fresh basil
Salt and pepper to taste
3 pounds crab meat

- ♦ Preheat oven to 325°
- ♦ Melt 1½ sticks butter in a sauce pan. Add flour and stir in half and half until thickened. Stir in Sherry.
- ♦ In a skillet melt the ½ stick butter. Add mushrooms and spinach and just lightly sautee. Add basil, salt and pepper. Stir into white sauce.
- ♦ Spread crab meat evenly in middle of each crepe. Pour some of sauce over crab. Roll crepe. Place on baking dish.
- ♦ Bake for 15 minutes or until just warmed.
- ♦ Remove from oven. Serve on plates with warm mushroom sauce.

*Crepes*

Makes about 20

4 eggs
2 cups milk
6 Tbls. butter, melted

1 cup flour
¼ cup chives, snipped

- ♦ Combine the ingredients in a bowl.
- ♦ Heat a crepe pan or small skillet. Add a dollop of butter.
- ♦ Spoon about 2 Tbls. batter into pan, turning pan so that batter is spread evenly. Brown for about 1 minute on each side.

# CRAB PIE

Serves 4

1 ½ cups half and half
3 eggs
¼ teaspoon cayenne
½ pound Gruyere

¼ pound country ham, cut into strips
1 pound crab meat
1 cup leeks, chopped

- ◆ Preheat oven to 400°
- ◆ Place the pie crust in the oven for 10 minutes. Remove from oven and place cheese and ham on crust. Top with crab and leeks.
- ◆ In a bowl beat the half and half, eggs and cayenne. Pour over crab. Bake 45 minutes or until set.

*Pie Crust*

1¼ cups flour
1 stick butter

¼ cup cold water
½ teaspoon salt

- ◆ Combine all ingredients in food processor. Roll out on floured board to fit pie plate.

# CRAB QUICHE

Serves 4

1 pound crab meat
1 cup Swiss cheese, grated
½ cup parmesan cheese, grated
1½ cups half and half

3 eggs
½ teaspoon nutmeg
Pie crust – see recipe above

- ◆ Preheat oven to 400°
- ◆ Place the pie crust in the oven for 10 minutes. Remove from oven and place crab and cheeses on crust.
- ◆ In a bowl beat the half and half, eggs and nutmeg. Pour over crab. Bake 45 minutes or until set.

# SEAFOOD CREPES

Serves 10 (2 crepes each)

Crepes (see p
2 sticks butter
1 cup flour
4 cups half and half
½ cup Sherry
1 cup parmesan cheese

1 pound mushrooms, sliced
5 green onions, sliced
2 pound crab meat
1 ½ pounds small shrimp
Parsley
Lemon slices

- ◆ Preheat oven to 325°
- ◆ Melt 1½ sticks butter in a sauce pan. Add flour and stir in half and half until thickened. Stir in Sherry and cheese.
- ◆ In a skillet melt the ½ stick butter. Add mushrooms and green onion and just lightly saute.
- ◆ Spread crab meat and shrimp evenly in middle of each crepe. Pour some of sauce over crab and shrimp. Roll crepe. Place on baking dish. Pour remaining sauce over crepes.
- ◆ Bake for 15 minutes or until just warmed.
- ◆ Remove from oven. Serve on plates and garnish with parsley and lemon slices/

# SMOKED SALMON TART

Serves 4

Pie Crust – p 183
1 pound smoked salmon
¼ cup fresh dill, snipped
1 cup leeks, chopped

1 8 oz. package cream cheese
1½ cups half and half
2 eggs

- ◆ Preheat oven to 400°
- ◆ Place the pie crust in the oven for 10 minutes. Remove from oven and place salmon, dill and leeks on crust. Spread with cream cheese
- ◆ In a bowl beat the half and half and eggs. Pour over cheese. Bake 45 minutes or until set.

# LEEK AND BACON TART

Serves 4

1 pie crust – p 183
6 slices bacon, cooked and crumbled
1 cup leeks, chopped

1 cup Swiss cheese, grated
3 eggs
1 ½ cups half and half

- ◆ Preheat oven to 400°
- ◆ Place the pie crust in the oven for 10 minutes. Remove from oven and place bacon, leeks and cheese on crust
- ◆ In a bowl beat the half and half and eggs. Pour over cheese. Bake 45 minutes or until set.


# POTATO FRITTATA

Serves 4

½ stick butter
8 eggs, beaten
4 slices cooked bacon, crumbled
4 small red potatoes, cooked and sliced
2 green onions, chopped

1 cup Monterey Jack cheese, grated
1 teaspoon pepper
½ teaspoon salt
¼ cup parsley
2 Tbls. dill, snipped

- ◆ Preheat oven to 400°
- ◆ In a large iron skillet melt the butter. Add eggs. Using spatula, keep eggs from sticking to pan. Cook for several minutes until almost set. Place the other ingredients on eggs.
- ◆ Put in oven. Bake 15 minutes or until just browned.

# VEGETABLE FRITTATA

Serves 4

½ stick butter
1 small zucchini, sliced
2 green onions, chopped
½ pound mushrooms, sliced
8 eggs, beaten

1 large tomato, sliced
1 teaspoon Italian herbs
½ pound Monterrey Jack cheese, grated

- ◆ Preheat the oven to 400°
- ◆ In an iron skillet melt the butter. Add the zucchini, onions and mushrooms. Stir until just tender.
- ◆ Pour the eggs over vegetables.
- ◆ Top with tomato slices, herbs and cheese.
- ◆ Bake for 15-20 minutes, until eggs are set.
- ◆ Slice and serve warm.

# ASPARAGUS FRITTATA

Serves 4

½ stick butter
8 eggs, beaten
2 green onions, chopped

½ pound spring asparagus, cut in
2 inch pieces
2 Tbls. dill
1 cup Gruyere cheese, grated

- ◆ Preheat oven to 400°
- ◆ In a large iron skillet melt the butter. Add eggs. Using spatula, keep eggs from sticking to pan. Cook for several minutes until almost set. Place the other ingredients on eggs.
- ◆ Put in oven. Bake 15 minutes or until just browned.

# EGG CASSEROLE

Serves 4

1 stick butter
½ cup flour
2 cups half and half
¼ cup Sherry
8 hardboiled eggs
½ pound mushrooms, sliced

1 cup fresh peas
2 green onion, chopped
½ red bell pepper, chopped
¼ cup fresh basil, chopped
1 cup parmesan cheese

- ♦ Preheat oven to 350°
- ♦ Melt the butter in a sauce pan. Add flour and half and half until thickened. Add Sherry.
- ♦ Place the eggs, mushrooms, peas, green onion, pepper and basil in greased casserole. Top with sauce and cheese.
- ♦ Bake 20 minutes or until just browned and bubbling.

# PANCAKES WITH ORANGE SAUCE

1 cup flour
¼ cup sugar
3 eggs, beaten
1 cup milk

1 teaspoon baking powder
2 Tbs. butter, melted
Zest of one orange

- ♦ Combine all ingredients in a bowl.
- ♦ Melt butter in a skillet. Fry pancakes and brown on each side.

*Orange Sauce*

½ cup sugar
1 ½ teaspoons cornstarch

1 cup orange juice
1 orange, peeled, and sliced

- ♦ Combine ingredients in a sauce pan. Stir until thickened. Serve over pancakes.

# BACON PANCAKE

Serves 4

4 strips bacon
3 eggs, beaten
2 cups milk
¼ cup sugar

1 teaspoon baking powder
1 green onion, chopped
½ red bell pepper, chopped

- ◆ Preheat oven to 400°
- ◆ Cook bacon in an iron skillet. Remove bacon and chop up. Save drippings in skillet. Put bacon back in the pan.
- ◆ In a bowl combine the other ingredients.
- ◆ Pour over bacon.
- ◆ Bake ½ hour or until just browned.
- ◆ Serve with lingonberry sauce, p.209

# PEACH PANCAKES

Makes about 8 pancakes

1 egg
1 cup milk
¼ cup sour cream
1 cup flour
¼ teaspoon salt
¼ cup sugar

1 Tbls. baking powder
½ stick butter, melted
2 peaches, peeled, pitted and sliced
Pecan butter
Maple syrup

- ◆ In a bowl beat the egg, milk and sour cream. Add flour, salt, sugar, baking powder and 2 Tbls. butter.
- ◆ In a skillet melt rest of butter. Saute peaches in butter, 1 minute on each side. Remove from skillet.
- ◆ If necessary add more butter to skillet. Drop pancake batter by large spoonfuls. Brown on each side.
- ◆ Serve with peaches, pecan butter and maple syrup.
- ◆ Pecan butter – soften 1 stick butter. Add ½ cup broken pecans.

# FRENCH TOAST

Makes 8 slices

8 thick slices French bread
4 eggs, beaten
2 cups half and half
1 teaspoon cinnamon

¼ cup sugar
1 teaspoon vanilla
1 cup pecans

- ♦ Beat the eggs, half and half, cinnamon, and sugar.
- ♦ Put the bread in a greased baking dish. Top with egg mixture and pecans. Let set overnight.
- ♦ Preheat oven to 400°
- ♦ Bake for ¾ hour or until just browned.
- ♦ Serve with maple syrup and butter.

# WELSH RAREBIT

Serves 4

8 toast, cut on diagonal
1 pound Stilton cheese
¾ cup milk
1 teaspoon Worcestershire sauce
1 teaspoon dry mustard

1 teaspoon paprika
Dash of cayenne
1 egg, beaten
1 cup beer

- ♦ In a sauce pan heat the cheese and milk over low heat until cheese is melted. Add Worcestershire, mustard, paprika and cayenne. Stir in egg and then beer.
- ♦ Pour cheese mixture over toast, two to a plate.

# SANDWICHES

Table set for tea

*"I dined at the Cocoa Tree....That respectable body affords every evening a sight truly English. Twenty or thirty of the first men in the kingdom....supping at little tables....upon a bit of cold meat, or a Sandwich."*

The first written record of the word 'sandwich', from Edward Gibbons Journal, 11/24/1762

# CRAB QUESADILLAS

Makes 8

1 pound crab meat
2 jalapenos, seeded and chopped
¼ cup cilantro, chopped
1 15 oz. can black beans,
drained
2 large tomatoes, chopped

1 cup fresh corn
4 green onions, chopped
½ pound Monterrey Jack cheese,
grated
8 tortillas

- ◆ Preheat oven to 400°
- ◆ In a bowl combine the crab, jalapenos, cilantro, beans, tomatoes, corn, and onions. Divide among the tortillas, placing amount on ½ tortilla. Top with cheese. Fold other half of tortilla over.
- ◆ Bake 10 minutes.

# CRAB SANDWICH

Serves 4

¼ cup mayonnaise
¼ cup sour cream
2 green onions, chopped
Juice of 1 lemon
8 slices herb bread

1 pound crab meat
4 slices tomato
1 cup Monterrey Jack cheese,
grated

- ◆ In a bowl combine the mayonnaise, sour cream, onion and lemon.
- ◆ Divide among 4 slices of bread. Top with crab, tomato and cheese. Put other slice on top. Cut in half.

# CRAB BLT

Serves 4

4 crab cakes
4 Boston lettuce leaves
4 slices tomato
4 slices bacon, cooked

Mayonnaise
Portuguese or sourdough large
rolls

♦ Put a small amount of mayonnaise on each roll.  Top with crab
cake, lettuce, tomato and bacon.

# CRAB AND SHRIMP

Serves 4

1 pound crab meat
½ pound small shrimp
1 8 oz package cream cheese
¼ cup dill

2 green onions
8 slices cheddar cheese
4 English muffins, cut in half

♦ Turn on broiler.
♦ In a bowl combine crab, shrimp, cream cheese, dill and onions.
♦ Place English muffins on a cookie sheet. Spread mixture on
muffins. Top with cheese.
♦ Broil until just browned and bubbling.

# CRAB SANDWICH

Serves 4

8 slices herb bread
Blue cheese dressing, p.209
1 pound crab meat

2 avocado, peeled, pitted and
sliced
1 cup bean sprouts

♦ Spread 4 slices of the bread with blue cheese dressing.
♦ Divide crab, avocado and sprouts between slices. Top with other
slice of bread.

# CRAB SANDWICH

Serves 4

1 pound crab meat
1 cup cheddar cheese, grated
½ cup mayonnaise
2 avocados, peeled, pitted and sliced

4 Boston lettuce leaves
4 slices tomato
4 sourdough bread or rolls

- ♦ In a bowl combine the crab, cheese and mayonnaise.
- ♦ Slice each roll in half. Spread the crab mixture on roll. Top with avocado, lettuce and tomato.

# ROCKFISH SANDWICH

Serves 4

Thousand Island Dressing
4 grilled rockfish filets
4 slices Swiss cheese

2 green onions, chopped
4 Boston lettuce leaves
Sourdough Rolls

- ♦ Put some of the dressing on each roll. Top with rockfish, cheese, onions and lettuce.

# CHICKEN PESTO

Serves 4

2 large grilled boneless chicken breasts, sliced
Mayonnaise

Pesto, p. 201
Baby spinach
8 slices herb bread

- ♦ Spread 4 slices of bread with a small amount of mayonnaise. Spread the other 4 slices with pesto. Top mayonnaise slice with chicken and spinach. Top with other slice.

# CHICKEN AND WATERCRESS SANDWICHES

Serves 4

8 slices herb bread
½ stick butter, softened
2 bunches watercress

Mayonnaise
2 large grilled boneless chicken breasts, sliced

- ◆ Spread butter on each bread slice. Top with a small amount of mayonnaise. Divide chicken and watercress between 4 sandwiches.
- ◆ Also can be made as tea sandwiches on thin white bread and rolled.


# GRILLED CHICKEN SANDWICHES

Serves 4

2 large grilled boneless chicken breasts, sliced
4 slices cooked bacon

Sliced smoked gouda cheese
BBQ sauce, heated p. 210
4 large rolls

- ◆ Place some of the chicken, bacon and cheese on each roll. Top with BBQ sauce.
- ◆ Cheddar cheese can be substituted for the smoked gouda.
- ◆ Pepper parmesan dressing, p 209 can be substituted for BBQ sauce.

# GRILLED CHICKEN SANDWICH

Makes 4

2 large grilled boneless chicken
breasts, sliced
4 slices smoked bacon, cooked
and crumbled
Guacamole, p. 200

4 slices tomato
4 lettuce leaves
Mayonnaise
8 slices herb bread

- ♦ Spread a small amount of mayonnaise on 4 slices bread. Spread guacamole on 4 other slices.
- ♦ On four slices divide chicken and bacon. Top with tomato slice and lettuce. Top with other slices of bread.

# GRILLED CHICKEN FAJITA

4 fajitas

2 Tbls. olive oil
1 large onion, sliced
1 red pepper, sliced
1 yellow pepper sliced
2 jalapenos, seeded and sliced
2 large boneless grilled chicken
breasts, sliced

1 cup Monterrey Jack cheese,
grated
4 warm tortillas
Sour cream
Salsa, p.199
Guacamole, p.200

- ♦ Heat the olive oil in a skillet. Add onion and peppers, sautéing until onion is transparent. Add chicken.
- ♦ Place some of chicken mixture on each tortilla. Top with cheese. Fold sides over.
- ♦ Serve with sour cream, guacamole and salsa.
- ♦ Grilled beef or shrimp can be substituted for the chicken

# CHICKEN CALZONE

*Dough*

3½ cups flour
1 package dry yeast
1 cup lukewarm water

1 Tbls. olive oil
1 teaspoon kosher salt

- ◆ Preheat oven to 500°
- ◆ Soften yeast in a cup of water.
- ◆ Place all ingredients in food processor until ball forms.
- ◆ Let the dough rise for one hour in oiled bowl
- ◆ Oil a cookie sheet and flatten dough on sheet. Let rise 1 more hour.

*Filling*

2 grilled boneless chicken
breasts, cubed
2 large tomatoes, chopped
¼ pound baby spinach

2 cups mozzarella
1 Tbls. oregano
3 cloves garlic, minced

- ◆ Combine all ingredients in a bowl.
- ◆ Spread filling down middle of dough.
- ◆ Fold sides over and seal sides and ends. Brush with 1 beaten egg.
- ◆ Bake 20 minutes or until browned.
- ◆ Serve hot or cold.

# CHICKEN SALAD

Serves 4

2 large grilled boneless chicken
breasts, cubed
¼ cup mayonnaise
¼ cup sour cream
½ cup toasted sunflower seeds

¼ cup basil, chopped
Salt and pepper to taste
4 leaves Boston lettuce
4 slices tomato
4 large rolls

- ◆ In a bowl combine the chicken, mayonnaise, sour cream, sunflower seeds, basil and salt and pepper.
- ◆ Spread mixture on roll. Top with lettuce and tomato.

# SAUSAGE PIZZA

Dough, p.194
½ pound sliced pepperoni
1 medium onion, chopped
½ red bell pepper, chopped
½ yellow pepper, chopped

½ pound mushrooms, sliced
½ pound sausage, cooked
½ pound ground beef, cooked
1 jar tomato marinara sauce
1 cup mozzarella cheese, grated

- ◆ Preheat oven to 500°
- ◆ Place all the pepperoni, onion, peppers, mushrooms, sausage and ground beef on dough, leaving 1 inch edge all around. Top with marinara sauce and cheese.
- ◆ Bake 20 minutes or until dough is just browned.

# VEGGIE PIZZA

Dough, p. 194
3 large tomatoes, thinly sliced
1 red bell pepper, chopped
1 yellow pepper, chopped
1 large onion, sliced and sauted

1 cup black olives
2 cups mozzarella or feta cheese
1 Tbls. oregano, chopped
¼ cup basil

- ◆ Preheat oven to 500°
- ◆ Spread the tomatoes on pizza dough. Top with other ingredients.
- ◆ Bake 20 minutes, or until dough is just slightly browned.

# SAUCES, CONDIMENTS AND RELISHES

Rigged for Oystering

# GREEN TOMATO RELISH

6 pounds ripe tomatoes, chopped
¼ cup salt
2 pounds onions, chopped
3 red peppers, chopped
3 yellow peppers, chopped
2 celery stalks, chopped
1 cup sugar

2 teaspoons celery seed
2 teaspoons mustard seed
2 teaspoons dry mustard
2 teaspoons cinnamon
1 teaspoon allspice
½ teaspoon ground cloves
2 cups cider vinegar

- ◆ Combine the ingredients in a large pot. Bring to a boil. Reduce heat and simmer for about 5 minutes.
- ◆ Ladle relish into sterilized jars.

# CORN RELISH

10 cups fresh corn
2 large onions, chopped
1 red pepper, chopped
1 green pepper, chopped
1 pound brown sugar

3 teaspoons celery seed
3 teaspoons mustard seed
2 Tbls. salt
4 cups cider vinegar

- ◆ Combine the ingredients in a large pot. Bring to a boil. Simmer for 15 minutes.
- ◆ Pour into sterilized jars.

# TOMATO SALSA

2 large ripe tomatoes, finely chopped
Juice of 1 lime
2 Tbls. olive oil
2 jalapeno, seeded and finely chopped

¼ cup cilantro, chopped
1 teaspoon salt
1 teaspoon fresh ground pepper
2 cloves garlic, minced
1 green onion, chopped

- ◆ Combine all the ingredients in a bowl.

# PEACH CHUTNEY

8 pounds ripe peaches, peeled, pitted, and chopped
4 cups brown sugar, packed
2 cups cider vinegar
1 medium onion, chopped
2 cups raisins or currants
4 apples, peeled, cored and chopped

2 Tbls. mustard seed
¼ cup fresh grated ginger
1 Tbls. salt
2 teaspoons paprika
2 teaspoons cumin
½ cup lime juice
Zest of 1 lime

- ♦ Combine all the ingredients in a large pot. Bring to a boil. Simmer 2 hours or until thickened.
- ♦ Pour into sterilized jars. Store in cool place.

# CUCUMBER SAUCE

Serve with salmon or other fish

Makes about 2 ½ cups sauce

2 cups sour cream
2 green onions, chopped
1 medium cucumber, peeled and finely chopped

Salt and pepper
Juice of 1 lemon
¼ cup fresh dill, snipped

- ♦ Combine all ingredients in a bowl.

# GUACAMOLE

2 large ripe avocados, peeled, pitted and chopped
¼ cup sour cream
2 Tbls. mayonnaise
1 teaspoon cumin

2 green onions, chopped
½ teaspoon salt
2 Tbls. lemon juice
3 cloves garlic, minced
1 teaspoon chili powder

- ♦ Combine all the ingredients in a bowl.

# EASY HOLLANDAISE

1 stick butter                    Juice of ½ lemon
3 egg yolks

- Melt butter in a small saucepan.
- Into food processor put egg yolks. Blend until smooth.
- Slowly pour butter into processor while blending.
- Add juice of the lemon.
- Serve with broccoli, fish, or on Eggs Benedict.

# PESTO

2 large bunches basil leaves      4 cloves garlic
½ cup olive oil                    ½ cup grated Parmesan cheese
½ cup pine nuts               Salt and pepper

- Place the ingredients in a food processor until just blended.

# HORSERADISH SAUCE

Serve with lamb, beef or pork roasts.

½ cup sour cream            ½ cup horseradish
½ cup heavy cream

- Combine the ingredients in a bowl.

# BEARNAISE SAUCE

2 Tbls. white wine vinegar
2 tablespoons white wine
1 tablespoon chopped shallots
1 tablespoon fresh tarragon

1 stick butter
3 egg yolks
½ lemon
Salt and pepper

- Melt the butter and pour into a food processor. Add egg yolks and lemon juice.
- Combine the vinegar, white wine, shallots and tarragon in a small saucepan. Bring to a boil and reduce to about half.
- Add to food processor mixture. Season with salt and pepper.
- Serve the sauce in a bowl with beef or pork tenderloin.

# SAUCE BEARNAISE

1 stick butter
3 egg yolks
¼ cup fresh lemon juice
2 Tbls. fresh tarragon

2 Tbls. fresh chervil
2 Tbls. shallots, chopped
¼ cup tarragon vinegar
¼ cup white wine

- Melt the butter in a sauce pan. In a food processor combine the butter, egg yolks and lemon juice.
- In a skillet warm the tarragon, chervil, shallots, vinegar and wine until liquid is reduced to one-half. Pour into the food processor and combine ingredients.

# DILL SAUCE

Delicious on salmon or other fish

1 cup sour cream
½ cup mayonnaise
2 Tbls. horseradish

¼ cup fresh dill, snipped
2 Tbls. capers

- Combine all the ingredients in a bowl.

# MUSTARD SAUCE FOR HAM

¼ cup Dijon mustard
1 cup sour cream
¼ cup brown sugar

2 Tbls. Worcestershire sauce
2 Tbls. horseradish

♦ Combine all ingredients in a bowl.


# MUSTARD SAUCE FOR FISH

¼ cup Dijon mustard
2 Tbls. sugar
2 Tbls. vinegar

¼ cup dill, snipped
1 cup olive oil

♦ Combine all ingredients in a food processor. Serve in a bowl with grilled fish.


# REMOULADE

This is very good with grilled fish.

1 cup mayonnaise
1 teaspoon dry mustard
Juice of 1 lemon
2 cloves garlic, minced

2 Tbls. capers
2 Tbls. tarragon, chopped
2 Tbls. parsley, chopped
1 hard-cooked egg, chopped
¼ teaspoon cayenne

♦ Combine all ingredients in a bowl

# GREEN SAUCE FOR FISH

2 bunches watercress
½ pound baby spinach
2 cups mayonnaise
1 cup sour cream

Juice of 1 lemon
3 cloves garlic
salt and pepper
¼ cup fresh dill

♦ Combine all ingredients in a food processor

# ORANGE SAUCE

1 cup orange juice
¼ cup Cointreau
2 Tbls. Dijon mustard

½ cup brown sugar
1 cup orange marmalade

Combine all ingredients in a sauce pan. Stir until slightly thickened.

# ORANGE SAUCE

Zest of 2 oranges
1 cup orange juice
1 Tbls. lemon juice
¼ cup Cointreau

1 Tbls. fresh grated ginger
½ cup sugar
2 teaspoons cornstarch

Combine all ingredients in a sauce pan. Stir until thickened.

# APRICOT SAUCE

1 cup apricot preserves
1 teaspoon dry mustard
½ teaspoon Worcestershire sauce

Juice of 1 lemon
Zest of 1 lemon
1 Tbls. horseradish
1 cup white wine

♦ Combine all ingredients in a sauce pan. Bring to a boil. Stir until slightly thickened.

# WILD MUSHROOM GRAVY

Serve with turkey or chicken

½ stick butter
¼ cup flour
1 cup half and half
1 cup chicken or turkey stock

½ pound fresh wild mushrooms, quartered
2 green onions, chopped
2 Tbls. fresh tarragon
½ cup sour cream

♦ Melt the butter in a sauce pan. Add flour and stir in half and half and stock. Fold in mushrooms, green onions, and tarragon. Just before serving add sour cream.

# MARINADE FOR PORK

½ cup soy sauce
¼ cup lemon juice
1 cup brown sugar
¼ cup olive oil

½ teaspoon cayenne
4 cloves garlic, minced
1 Tbls. fresh ground pepper
¼ cup ketchup

♦ Combine all ingredients in a sauce pan. Bring to a boil. Simmer until thickened.

# APPLE SAUCE

Serve with pork.

½ pound dried apricots
2 large apples, peeled and chopped
¼ cup brown sugar

½ cup vinegar
2 Tbls. fresh ginger, chopped
½ cup almonds
¼ teaspoon cayenne

♦ Combine all ingredients in a sauce pan. Bring to a boil. Let simmer 1 hour.

# GRAND MARNIER SAUCE

1 Tbls. vinegar
½ cup sugar
1 cup fresh orange juice
½ cup Grand Marnier

Zest of 2 oranges
Pan juices
Orange slices from 2 oranges

Cook the vinegar and sugar in a sauce pan until sugar carmelizes. Add orange juice, Grand Marnier and zest. Stir in pan juices from duck or goose.
Serve with duck or goose and garnish with orange slice garnish.

# GARLIC AOLI

½ cup mayonnaise
¼ cup milk

Juice of 1 lemon
2 cloves garlic, minced

♦ Combine ingredients in a bowl.

# STILTON CHEESE DRESSING

1 cup Stilton
½ cup mayonnaise
¼ cup white wine vinegar
2 Tbls. sugar

½ cup sour cream
2 cloves garlic, minced
2 chives, snipped

- ♦ Combine ingredients in a bowl.
- ♦ Blue cheese can be substituted for the Stilton.

# SWEET VIDALIA ONION DRESSING

1 medium Vidalia onion, chopped
½ cup olive oil
¼ cup tarragon vinegar

½ teaspoon paprika
½ teaspoon salt
¼ teaspoon cayenne

- ♦ Combine the ingredients in a food processor.

# TOMATO BASIL VINAIGRETTE

4 shallots
¼ cup balsamic vinegar
½ teaspoon salt

½ cup olive oil
¼ cup basil, chopped
1 large tomato chopped

- ♦ Combine all ingredients in a food processor.

# ROASTED GARLIC LEMON VINAIGRETTE

4 garlic heads
2 Tbls. olive oil
2 Tbls. water

½ cup lemon juice
½ cup olive oil

- ♦ Preheat oven to 350°
- ♦ Remove the outer paper skin from garlic.
- ♦ Brush baking dish with olive oil and water. Place garlic on dish.
- ♦ Bake 1 hour. You may need to add more water.
- ♦ Remove garlic and put through a food mill. Discard skins.
- ♦ In a jar combine the garlic, lemon juice and ¼ cup olive oil for vinaigrette.

# BALSAMIC VINAIGRETTE

½ cup olive oil
¼ cup balsamic vinegar
1 Tbls. Dijon mustard

½ teaspoon kosher salt
1 teaspoon fresh ground pepper

- ♦ Combine ingredients in bowl.

# WHITE WINE SAUCE

½ stick butter
¼ cup flour

1 cup half and half
½ cup dry white wine

- ♦ Melt butter in sauce pan. Gradually add flour and then half and half until thickened. Stir in white wine.

# LINGONBERRY SAUCE

½ cup Port
½ cup orange juice
¼ cup lemon juice

½ cup lingonberry jelly
2 Tbls. orange zest
2 Tbls. lemon zest

Combine ingredients in a sauce pan. Bring to a boil. Simmer 5 minutes. Let thicken.

# BLUE CHEESE DRESSING

1 cup blue cheese or gorgonzola, crumbled
1 cup mayonnaise
1 cup sour cream

¼ cup tarragon vinegar
2 Tbls. sugar
2 cloves garlic, minced
2 chives, snipped

♦ Combine all ingredients in a bowl.

# PEPPER PARMESAN SAUCE

½ stick butter
¼ cup flour
1 cup milk

1 cup parmesan cheese
1 Tbls. fresh ground pepper

♦ Melt the butter in a sauce pan. Add flour and stir in milk. Add cheese and pepper.

# BBQ SAUCE

½ cup ketchup
¼ cup vinegar
2 Tbls. brown sugar
¼ cup water
1 Tbls. Worcestershire sauce
2 Tbls. lemon juice

2 green onions, chopped
3 cloves garlic, minced
2 teaspoons dry mustard
¼ teaspoon cayenne
1 teaspoon Old Bay or Wye River seasoning

- ♦ Combine all the ingredients in a sauce pan. Cook until thickened, about 20 minutes.
- ♦ Place in a jar and refrigerate overnight before using.
- ♦ Can be served hot or chilled.

# HOT FUDGE SAUCE

4 ounces unsweetened chocolate
½ stick butter
1 cup sugar

1 cup heavy cream
1 teaspoon vanilla

- ♦ Combine all the ingredients in a sauce pan.

# RUM RAISIN SAUCE

This is delicious served over ice cream.

½ cup dark rum
½ cup raisins
½ cup water
1 teaspoon cinnamon

1 teaspoon vanilla
2 Tbls. orange juice
Zest of 1 orange
½ cup chopped pecans

- ♦ Combine all ingredients in a sauce pan. Bring to a boil. Simmer 5 minutes.
- ♦ Store in a sealed glass jar.

# DESSERTS

Bowl of strawberries for a spring dessert

*"The wisest choice of dessert is one that is confined to ripe cheese, preserves, and wines that are dry, old, and warm, like sherry. La Chapelle, major-domo of Louis XIII, was of the opinion that any man who sets store by a dessert after a good dinner is a madman who allows his judgment to be affected by his stomach! . . . . The best desserts consist of well-flavored good foods that do not cake long to eat. What could be more suitable than cheese? . . . Take care not to introduce a new course with gâteaux and sweetmeats, which would be bad for digestion, only out of sheer gluttony! However, we are not dogmatic, and we offer the ladies (after the ices) petits fours, morello cherries, and other delicacies."* Maurice des Ombiaux, 'Traite de la table'

For those of you sailors dessert was always known as "afters" when at sea.

Governor William Bladen of Maryland was known to have enjoyed strawberry ice cream in 1770.

In 1784 George Washington purchased a "cream machine for ice". During an inventory at Mount Vernon in the 1800s two "pewter ice cream pots" were mentioned.

Ice creams ads appeared in Maryland papers as early as 1798.

The hand-cranked ice cream freezer was patented in 1848 by

Ice cream molds also became popular in the 19th c. Everything from swans to boats and flowers arrived on tables, made by an industrious housewife. Later they were made in bake shops or ice cream shops.

Jacob Fussell began making ice cream in 1851 in a building at Hillen and Exeter Streets in Baltimore. By 1856 he also had opened ice cream parlors in Boston and Washington. A Centennial Celebration was held in 1951 to celebrate the "birthplace of the ice cream industry". Tony Curtis and Piper Laurie were crowned "Sweethearts of the Ice Cream Industry". This was organized by Manuel Hendler.

The Hendler Ice Cream Company, Baltimore was established in 1912 in a state of the art factory on E. Baltimore Street. The first flavors were vanilla, chocolate and strawberry. Their ice cream was billed as the "The Velvet Kind" ice cream. Hendler's supplied the ginger ice cream for the old Hutzler's department store tearoom. The company was bought by Borden c1932 and unfortunately went out of business in the 1960s.

In the early 1900s Marion, Maryland was the largest shipper of strawberries in the world! Hundreds of refrigerated railroad cars left the Marion Train Station each day. Sadly by the 1950s the industry died out. Corn and soy beans took over as dominant crops in this lower part of the Eastern Shore of Maryland.

# STRAWBERRY SHORTCAKE

Serves 6

| | |
|---|---|
| 1 quart strawberries, sliced | ¼ cup Grand Marnier |
| 1 ½ cups whipping cream | Shortcakes |
| ½ cup sugar | |

Cut shortcakes in two. Place some of the strawberries inside. Top with more strawberries. Top with whipped cream mixture.
Whip cream in a bowl until peaks form. Add sugar and Grand Marnier.

*Shortcakes*

| | |
|---|---|
| 1 stick butter | ¾ cup half and half |
| 2 cups flour | ½ teaspoon cinnamon |
| ½ cup sugar | 3 teaspoons baking powder |

- ♦ Preheat oven to 400°
- ♦ Combine all ingredients in a food processor until a ball forms. Roll out on a floured board. Cut with large biscuit cutter. Place on cookie sheet.
- ♦ Bake 12 minutes, or until browned.

# CUBAN STRAWBERRIES

This is a Cuban dish from my niece Gaby's mother

| | |
|---|---|
| 1 quart strawberries, sliced | ¼ cup balsamic vinegar |

- ♦ Combine the ingredients in a bowl.

# STRAWBERRY MOUSSE

Serves 4-6

1 envelope gelatin
½ cup water
1 cup sugar
2 cups heavy cream, whipped

1 pint strawberries, sliced
½ cup slivered almonds
¼ cup Grand Marnier

- Dissolve the gelatin in a bowl with the water.
- In a bowl combine the gelatin and sugar. Fold in the cream, strawberries, almonds, and Grand Marnier. Place in soufflé dish.
- Put in freezer for at least 2 hours. Serve with strawberry sauce
- Raspberries can be substituted for the strawberries

*Strawberry Sauce*

1 pint strawberries
1 cup sugar

¼ cup Grand Marnier

- Combine the ingredients in a food processor.


# STRAWBERRY MOUSSE II

Serves 4

4 ounces white chocolate
1 cup sugar
½ cup water
1 package gelatin

1 quart strawberries
2 cups whipping cream,
whipped

- Melt the chocolate with the sugar in a sauce pan.
- Combine the water and gelatin in a cup.
- In a food processor combine the chocolate, gelatin and ½ the strawberries. Remove and put in a soufflé dish. Fold in whipping cream.
- Put in freezer or refrigerator for at least two hours.
- Garnish with remaining strawberries and more whipped cream if desired.

# STRAWBERRY CHEESECAKE

1½ cups graham cracker crumbs
½ cup toasted slivered almonds
½ stick butter, melted
¼ cup sugar
2 8 oz. packages cream cheese
1 cup sugar

2 eggs
Zest of 1 lemon
2 teaspoons vanilla
Juice of 1 lemon
1 pint strawberries

- ◆ Preheat oven to 350°
- ◆ In a bowl combine the cracker crumbs, butter, ¼ cup sugar, and almonds
- ◆ Press crumbs into a glass pie plate
- ◆ In a bowl beat together cream cheese, sugar, lemon juice, lemon peel, vanilla and eggs.
- ◆ Pour mixture into pie crust. Bake for 35 minutes.

*Glaze*

1 pint strawberries, sliced
1 cup strawberry jam

2 Tbls. Framboise liqueur

- ◆ Combine the ingredients in a sauce pan. Bring to a boil. Cool.
- ◆ Spread on cheesecake before serving.

# RASPBERRY PARFAIT

Serves 4

1 cup whipping cream
½ teaspoon almond extract
12 macaroons
1 pint vanilla ice cream

1 pint raspberry sherbet
1 pint raspberries
½ teaspoon nutmeg

- ◆ Beat the cream until peaks form. Add almond extract.
- ◆ Put 3 macaroons in the bottom of 4 parfait glasses. Top with some of each ice cream.
- ◆ Divide raspberries between glasses. Garnish with whipped cream and a small amount of nutmeg.

# RASPBERRY TRIFLE

Serves 12

1½ dozen ladyfingers
1 ½ dozen macaroons
1 cup Port
1 quart s raspberries

1 cup dried apricots
2½ cups heavy cream
1 cup toasted almonds

- ♦ In a large clear punch bowl arrange the ladyfingers and macaroons separately around the side of the bowl. Pour the Port over them so that it can be absorbed.
- ♦ Evenly distribute the fruit over the ladyfingers and macaroons (reserve several berries for garnish).
- ♦ Pour custard over the fruit. Refrigerate.
- ♦ Lightly whip the cream and spread over the custard.
- ♦ Garnish with almonds and extra raspberries.

*Custard*

8 egg yolks
¼ cup sugar

3½ cups heavy cream
1 teaspoon almond extract

- ♦ Whisk the egg yolks and sugar in a bowl.
- ♦ Bring the cream to a boil in a heavy sauce pan. Remove from heat.
- ♦ Slowly pour the egg mixture into the cream, stirring constantly with a wooden spoon.
- ♦ Return the pan to the stove and still stirring heat pan to thicken the custard. Do not allow to boil.
- ♦ Remove from heat and stir in almond extract. Refrigerate before using.

# RASPBERRY MOUSSE

Serves 6

1 envelope gelatin
½ cup orange juice
½ cup sugar
2 Tbls. Framboise liqueur

2 egg whites, beaten until stiff
1 ½ cups heavy cream whipped
2 pints fresh raspberries
Mint leaves

- In a bowl soften the gelatin in the orange juice. Stir in the sugar and Framboise.
- Fold in the egg whites, cream and 1½ pints raspberries.
- Pour into mold. Chill until firm or overnight.
- Unmold on plate. Garnish with rest of raspberries and mint.

# GRAND MARNIER SOUFFLE

Serves 4

3 eggs, separated
½ cup sugar
¼ cup Grand Marnier
1 cup whipping cream

1 teaspoon vanilla
1 envelope unflavored gelatin
¼ cup cold water
1 pint raspberries

- In a large bowl beat the egg yolks. Add the sugar and Grand Marnier.
- In another bowl beat the egg whites until stiff
- In another bowl beat the cream until peaks form. Add the vanilla.
- In a measuring cup dissolve the gelatin in the water.
- Stir gelatin mixture into egg yolks. Fold in egg whites, cream and ½ raspberries.
- Pour into soufflé bowl and chill overnight.

*Sauce*

½ pint raspberries
2 Tbls. Grand Marnier

¼ cup powdered sugar

- Combine the ingredients in a bowl. Serve over the soufflé.

217

# SYLLABUB

Serves 8

4 cups whipping cream            Zest of 2 oranges
1 cup sherry                      1 cup sugar
1 cup fresh orange juice

- Combine all ingredients.
- Pour a small amount of sherry into 8 martini glasses. Top with Cream mixture.
- Lemon juice and lemon zest can be substituted for the orange juice and zest.

# CHOCOLATE MOUSSE

Serves 6

8 oz. semi-sweet chocolate     ¼ cup dark rum
1 cup sugar                  2 cups whipping cream
2 Tbls. espresso coffee        4 eggs, separated

- In a sauce pan melt the chocolate with the sugar and coffee. Remove from heat and add rum and egg yolks.
- In a bowl beat whipping cream.
- In a separate bowl beat egg whites.
- Fold the whipped cream and egg whites into the chocolate mixture.
- Put in a soufflé dish and refrigerate for at least 2 hours.

*Raspberry Sauce*

2 pints raspberries           ¼ cup rum
¼ cup sugar

- Place 1 pint of the raspberries, sugar and rum in food processor. Puree.
- Serve mousse with sauce and garnish with raspberries.

# PUMPKIN MOUSSE

Serves 6-8

2 cups canned pumpkin
1 teaspoon cinnamon
½ teaspoon ginger
½ teaspoon nutmeg
½ teaspoon cloves
2 1 oz. envelopes gelatin

¼ cup rum
½ cup water
4 eggs, separated
1 cup sugar
1 cup heavy cream, whipped

- ♦ Combine pumpkin and spices in a bowl.
- ♦ Stir gelatin, rum and water in a pan until gelatin is dissolved.
- ♦ Beat egg whites until stiff.
- ♦ In separate bowl beat egg yolks and sugar. Add pumpkin and gelatin mixtures. Fold in whipped cream and egg whites.
- ♦ Pour into large soufflé dish. Refrigerate overnight.
- ♦ Serve with whipped cream and a dusting of cinnamon.

# GINGER DELIGHT

Serves 8

4 cups whipping cream
½ cup sugar
2 Tbls. ginger, grated

1 cup coconut
1 cup walnuts
1 cup dark rum
1 box ginger snaps

- ♦ Whip the cream with the sugar until peaks are formed. Fold in ginger, coconut, walnuts and rum.
- ♦ In a glass salad bowl place a layer of ginger snaps. Top with whipped cream mixture. Do another layer or two. Top with whipped cream mixture.
- ♦ Garnish with shredded coconut and more walnuts.
- ♦ Refrigerate and serve chilled.

# CHRISTMAS PUDDING

4 sticks butter
2 cups sugar
1 dozen eggs, separated
4 cups fine bread crumbs
2 cups raisins or currants

2 cups candied fruit
1 cup candied cherries
1 cup dates
1 cup brandy
1 teaspoon vanilla

- In a bowl soak the raisins, fruit, cherries, dates and brandy overnight, covered.
- In a bowl cream the butter and sugar. Beat in egg yolks.
- Beat egg whites in separate bowl and fold into butter mixture. Add bread crumbs and fruit. More brandy can be added.
- Pour into pudding molds or Pyrex bowls. Cover tightly with cheesecloth.
- Boil in a large kettle with water ¾ up to mold. Cook for at least 2 hours or until done.
- Keep in mold or bowl in refrigerator or cook place, occasionally pouring brandy or top.
- Nuts can also be added.
- When ready to serve heat and invert onto serving dish.
- Pour heated flamed brandy over pudding.

# CRÈME BRULEE

Serves 6

2 cups heavy cream
1 vanilla bean, split and remove seeds

6 ounces white chocolate
4 egg yolks
½ cup sugar

- Preheat oven to 325°.
- In a sauce pan heat the cream and beans for 3 minutes, or until bubbles form. Stir in chocolate. Remove from heat. Cool.
- In a bowl whisk the egg yolks and ¼ cup sugar. Stir in the chocolate mixture. Pour into 6 ramekins.
- Bake for 25-30 minutes or until set.
- Cool to room temperature and refrigerate for at least 4 hours.
- Remove from refrigerator and sprinkle the remaining sugar over each ramekin. Using a torch melt the sugar. Serve immediately.

# COFFEE ICE CREAM

Makes 1 quart

3 cups half and half
6 egg yolks
1 cup sugar
pinch of salt

¼ cup of your favorite ground coffee
1 teaspoon vanilla

- ♦ In a sauce pan warm the half and half until it steams.
- ♦ In a mixing bowl combine the egg yolks, sugar and salt. Gradually add the hot half and half.
- ♦ Put back in the sauce pan and stir with a wooden spoon until the mixture thickens.
- ♦ Stir in the coffee and vanilla.
- ♦ Place in an ice cream maker and follow directions. Refrigerate for at least 4 hours.

# SPICED PEACHES

Serves 6

6 large peaches, peeled, pitted and sliced
½ teaspoon cloves
1 teaspoon cinnamon

¼ pound crystallized ginger
¼ cup vinegar
½ cup sugar
1 cup dry white wine

- ♦ Combine all the ingredients in a sauce pan. Bring to a boil. Simmer for 5 minutes.
- ♦ Serve hot or chilled in bowls with whipped cream or ice cream.

# PEACH CRISP

Serves 6

6 ripe peaches, peeled, pitted
and sliced
Juice of 1 lemon
½ cup raisins
1 cup pecans
½ cup brown sugar
1 teaspoon cinnamon

½ teaspoon cloves
½ teaspoon ginger
½ teaspoon nutmeg
¼ cup flour
1 cup coconut
¼ cup oats
1 stick butter

- ♦ Preheat oven to 350°
- ♦ Arrange the peaches in large baking dish. Squeeze the lemon juice over the peaches. Stir in raisins and pecans.
- ♦ In a bowl combine all the other ingredients. Spoon onto peaches.
- ♦ Bake 45 minutes.
- ♦ Apples or pears can be substituted for peaches.


# PEACHES IN SHERRY

Serves 4

4 large peaches, peeled, pitted
and sliced
¼ cup Sherry
½ teaspoon cinnamon

¼ cup crystallized ginger
¼ cup toasted coconut
¼ cup toasted almonds

- ♦ In a bowl soak the peaches in the sherry, cinnamon and ginger. Serve in martini glasses topped with coconut and almonds.

# PEACH PIE

*Crust*

1 stick butter
1¼ cups flour
¼ cup cold water

3 Tbls. cream cheese
½ cup slivered almonds
½ teaspoon almond extract

- ♦ Preheat oven to 350°
- ♦ Place all the ingredients in a food processor until a ball forms.
- ♦ Roll out on floured board in shape of pie plate.

*Filling*

4 large ripe peaches, peeled,
pitted and sliced
½ cup brown sugar

1 Tbls. cornstarch
2 Tbls. lemon juice
½ teaspoon nutmeg

- ♦ Place the peaches in a circle in the pie plate.
- ♦ In a bowl combine the brown sugar, cornstarch, lemon juice and nutmeg. Pour over the peaches.
- ♦ Bake pie for 35-40 minutes, or until just slightly browned and bubbling.

*Topping*

½ cup flour
½ cup rolled oats
1 Tbls. cinnamon

¼ cup sugar
¼ cup brown sugar

- ♦ Combine the ingredients in a bowl. Spread over peaches.

# POACHED PEACHES

Serves 6

2 cups boiling water
1 cup sugar
Juice of 1 lemon
6 large peaches, peeled, pitted, and cut in half
½ stick butter
½ cup dark rum

¼ teaspoon nutmeg
1 teaspoon cinnamon
½ teaspoon ginger
Whipped cream or ice cream
Toasted pecans, almonds or walnuts

- In a sauce pan bring the water and sugar to a boil.
- Add lemon juice and peaches.
- Simmer for 15-20 minutes or until peaches are tender. If they are very ripe it might take less time. Remove peaches and place in a bowl
- Add butter, rum, and spices to sauce pan. Cook until butter has melted.
- Place 2 peach halves in each serving dish.
- Top with sauce. Serve with whipped cream or ice cream and nuts.

# BAKED PEARS

Serves 6

6 large ripe pears
1 cup orange juice
Zest of 2 oranges
¼ cup Cointreau

Juice of 1 lemon
¼ cup honey
Whipping cream

- Preheat oven to 300°
- Cut pears in half. Place cut side down in baking dish. Combine rest of ingredients, except cream in a bowl. Pour over pears.
- Bake for 20 minutes.
- Serve with whipped cream, crème fraiche or sour cream.

# ZABLAGLIONE WITH BERRIES

Serves 4

## *Zablaglione*

5 egg yolks, plus 1 whole egg        ½ cup Marsala
2 Tbls. sugar                        1 pint raspberries

- ♦ Combine the eggs and sugar in a double boiler. Simmer. Beat until fluffy. Slowly add Marsala.
- ♦ Serve in parfait glasses.
- ♦ Top with raspberries and sauce.

## *Cinnamon Custard*

2 egg yolks                          1 cup heavy cream
¼ cup sugar                          1 teaspoon cinnamon

- ♦ Whisk the egg yolks and sugar in a bowl.
- ♦ Bring the cream to a boil in a heavy sauce pan. Remove from heat.
- ♦ Slowly pour the egg mixture into the cream, stirring constantly with a wooden spoon.
- ♦ Return the pan to the stove and still stirring heat pan to thicken the custard. Do not allow to boil.
- ♦ Remove from heat and stir in cinnamon. Refrigerate before using.

# FRUIT COMPOTE

Serves

2 cups fresh pineapple
½ pound dried apricots
1 15 ounce can bing cherries
2 oranges, peeled and cut into sections
1 cup orange juice
½ cup honey

Zest of two oranges
1 teaspoon cinnamon
¼ cup crystalized ginger
½ stick butter, melted
Sour cream
Pistachios

- ◆ Preheat oven to 350°
- ◆ Arrange pineapple, apricots and bing cherries in a 2 quart baking dish.
- ◆ In a bowl combine orange juice, honey, zest, cinnamon and ginger. Pour over fruit.
- ◆ Bake 20 minutes, or until just warmed.
- ◆ Serve with sour cream and pistachios

# APPLE CAKE

1 stick butter
1 cup sugar
1 cup sour cream
2 eggs
2 cups flour
1 Tbls. baking powder

1 teaspoon cinnamon
2 Tbls. ground coffee
2 apples, peeled, cored and grated
1 cup walnuts

- ◆ Preheat oven to 350°
- ◆ Cream butter and sugar. Add sour cream and eggs. Beat in flour, baking powder, cinnamon and coffee. Stir in apples and walnuts.
- ◆ Pour into 9 x 13 greased baking dish.
- ◆ Bake 45 minutes.
- ◆ Serve with whipped cream, ice cream or cream cheese frosting.
- ◆ This can also be served as a breakfast coffee cake.

# APPLE CAKE

1½ stick butter
1 cup sugar
1 cup brown sugar
4 large apples, peeled and chopped
3 eggs
3 cups flour

1 Tbls. cinnamon
2 teaspoons nutmeg
1 teaspoon ginger
1 teaspoon allspice
1 teaspoon vanilla
1 cup pecans
2 teaspoons baking powder

- ◆ Preheat oven to 350°
- ◆ Cream butter and sugars. Add other ingredients. Pour into 9 x 13 greased baking dish or 2 9" cake pans.
- ◆ Bake 45 minutes.
- ◆ Serve with whipped cream, ice cream or cream cheese frosting.

# APPLE CRANBERRY PIE

9" pie crust

*Filling*

3 large apples, peeled, cored and thinly sliced
1 cup almonds
1 cup raisins
1 Tbls. grated orange rind
2 Tbls. bourbon
½ stick butter
¼ cup sugar

¼ cup brown sugar
¼ cup flour
½ teaspoon nutmeg
½ teaspoon ground ginger
1 Tbls. cinnamon
¼ teaspoon ground cloves
½ teaspoon ground allspice

- ◆ Preheat oven to 350°.
- ◆ Combine all the ingredients in a bowl.
- ◆ Pour ingredients into pie crust.
- ◆ Bake 45 minutes.
- ◆ Serve with ice cream or whipped cream.

# GINGERBREAD

1 stick butter
1 cup brown sugar
½ cup molasses
2 eggs
2 cups flour

2 teaspoons baking powder
2 teaspoons ginger
½ teaspoon nutmeg
2 Tbls. dark rum
½ cup coconut

- ◆ Preheat oven to 350°
- ◆ Cream butter and sugar. Add other ingredients.
- ◆ Pour into greased 9" baking dish.
- ◆ Bake for 30-35 minutes.
- ◆ Serve with hard sauce, whipped cream or ice cream.

# NUT CAKE

2 sticks butter, softened
2 cups sugar
6 eggs
2 cups flour

2 teaspoons baking powder
3 cups pecans
1 cup bourbon

- ◆ Preheat oven to 350°
- ◆ Cream the butter in a large bowl. Add sugar. Slowly add eggs, then flour and baking powder, always scrapping sides of bowl. Fold in nuts.
- ◆ Pour into bundt pan that has been greased and just lightly coated with flour. Put in oven.
- ◆ Place a baking sheet on a lower shelf. Pour in boiling water.
- ◆ Bake 1 ½ hours. Remove. Cool.
- ◆ Brush with bourbon. Wrap in cheesecloth and put in plastic zip bag. Keep basting with bourbon for several weeks.
- ◆ Serve in small slices.
- ◆ Whipped cream or ice cream can be served with the cake.
- ◆ Slivered almonds or walnuts can be substituted for the pecans

# BREAD PUDDING

Serves 6

1 cup brown sugar
1 ½ cups half and half
½ stick butter
1 teaspoon cinnamon
Zest of 1 orange
4 eggs, beaten

6 cups French bread cubes
1 cup almonds
½ cup raisins
1 apples, peeled, cored and chopped

- ♦ Preheat oven to 350°
- ♦ Heat first five ingredients in a sauce pan till boiling. Reduce heat and simmer for 5 minutes. Remove from heat. Add eggs.
- ♦ Layer rest of ingredients in greased baking dish. Pour sauce over top.
- ♦ Bake 30-35 minutes or until custard is set.

*Butterscotch Brandy Sauce*

3 egg yolks, beaten
1 stick butter
½ cup water

1 ½ cups brown sugar
1 cup light corn syrup
¼ cup brandy or rum

- ♦ Combine all ingredients, except brandy in sauce pan. Cook on low heat until thickened. Stir in brandy.

# SCONES

3 cups flour
¾ cup sugar
2 teaspoons baking powder
1 stick butter

¾ cup raisins
1 cup cream
2 eggs

- ♦ Preheat oven to 400°
- ♦ Combine all ingredients in a bowl.
- ♦ On a floured cutting board roll out the dough and with large biscuit cutter or into triangular shapes.
- ♦ Place on cookie and sheet and bake 15-20 minutes – light brown.

# POUND CAKE

2 sticks butter
3 cups sugar
6 eggs
3 cups flour

1 teaspoon vanilla
1 Tbls. almond flavoring or rum
½ cup almonds
1 cup heavy cream

- ♦ Preheat oven to 350°
- ♦ Cream butter and sugar. Add eggs one at a time along with flour. Add vanilla and almond flavoring. Add almonds and cream.
- ♦ Pour into greased loaf pan.
- ♦ Bake 1 hour.

# PEACH UPSIDE DOWN CAKE

2 sticks butter, melted
1 cup brown sugar
4 medium peaches, peeled, pitted and sliced
2 ½ cups flour
2 teaspoons baking powder
1 teaspoon cinnamon

1 teaspoon ginger
½ teaspoon cloves
½ cup molasses
½ cup honey
¾ cup hot water
1 egg
½ cup sugar

- ♦ Preheat oven to 350°
- ♦ Combine 1stick butter with the brown sugar in a bowl. Pat mixture into a greased 9x9 square glass baking dish.
- ♦ Arrange the peach slices, overlapping, on the brown sugar and butter mixture.
- ♦ In a bowl combine the other ingredients and the remaining butter. Pour the batter over the peaches.
- ♦ Bake 1 hour or until an inserted toothpick comes out dry.
- ♦ Pears, apples, pineapple or mangoes can be substituted for the peaches.

# BANANA TEMPURA

Serves 6

6 bananas, cut in half lengthwise
oil

Butter pecan ice cream
1 cup toasted coconut

- ◆ Coat each banana half with the batter.
- ◆ Heat the oil in a skillet. Fry the bananas until browned on all sides.
- ◆ Serve with butter pecan ice cream and coconut.

*Batter*

1 egg yolk
2 cups cold water
1 teaspoon baking powder

1¾ cup flour
½ cup sugar

- ◆ Combine the ingredients in a bowl.

# BANANA FRITTERS

Serves 6

6 large ripe bananas, cut in quarters, lengthwise
Flour

½ stick butter
½ cup dark rum

- ◆ Dip the bananas in flour and then batter.
- ◆ Melt the butter in a skillet. Cook the bananas until golden brown.
- ◆ Put on serving dish.
- ◆ Heat rum. Pour flaming over bananas.

*Batter*

½ cup flour
2 Tbls. melted butter
1 egg, beaten

½ cup beer
½ teaspoon cinnamon
2 egg whites, beaten till stiff

- ◆ Combine all ingredients, except egg white in a bowl.
- ◆ Let sit for 1 hour. Fold in egg whites.

# SWEET POTATO PIE

9"pie crust

3 eggs, beaten
2 cups sweet potatoes, cooked, peeled, and mashed
1 ½ cups sugar
2 Tbls. honey
1 cup half and half

½ stick butter
½ cup orange juice
1 teaspoon nutmeg
1 teaspoon baking powder
Nutmeg

- ♦ Preheat oven to 325°
- ♦ Combine all the ingredients, except nutmeg, in a bowl.
- ♦ Pour into pie crust. Bake 35 minutes.
- ♦ Garnish with nutmeg.


# SHOOFLY PIE

One of our favorite desserts growing up was shoofly pie.

1 cup flour
½ cup brown sugar
¼ cup Crisco
1 teaspoon baking soda

1 cup boiling water
¾ cup light corn syrup
¼ cup molasses
1 pie crust

- ♦ Preheat the oven to 375°

*Topping*

- ♦ Combine the flour, brown sugar and Crisco in a bowl so that it resembles coarse meal.

*Filling*

- ♦ In a bowl dissolve the baking soda in boiling water. Add the corn syrup and molasses.
- ♦ Pour the mixture into the pie crust.
- ♦ Sprinkle topping over mixture.
- ♦ Bake for 10 minutes. Reduce heat to 350°. Bake 25 minutes or until set. Cool.
- ♦ Serve with whipped cream or ice cream.

# BROWNIES

2 sticks butter
4 oz. dark chocolate
4 eggs

2 cups sugar
1 cup flour
1 teaspoon vanilla

♦ Preheat oven to 350°
♦ Melt the butter and chocolate in a saucepan.
♦ Stir in sugar, eggs, flour and vanilla.
♦ Bake in a 9" square pan for 30 minutes.
♦ Remove from oven and spread on topping. Put back in oven for 5 more minutes.

*Topping*

½ cup walnuts, pecans or peanuts
½ cup chocolate chips

½ cup miniature marshmallows
½ cup coconut

♦ Combine the ingredients in a bowl.


# CHOCOLATE COOKIES

1 stick butter
4 ounces unsweetened chocolate
1 ½ cups sugar
3 eggs
2 teaspoons baking powder

1 teaspoon vanilla
2 cups flour
1 cup walnuts or pecans
Powdered sugar

♦ Preheat oven to 375°
♦ Melt the butter and chocolate in a sauce pan. Remove from heat.
♦ Stir in rest of ingredients, except powdered sugar.
♦ Roll dough into 1 inch balls. Roll balls in powdered sugar.
♦ Bake on ungreased cookie sheet for 8-10 minutes. Cool. Sprinkle with more powdered sugar.

# CINNAMON COOKIES

1 stick butter
1 cup sugar
1½ cups flour
1 egg

1 teaspoon vanilla
1 teaspoon baking powder
1 Tbls. cinnamon

- ♦ Cream butter and sugar in bowl. Add rest of ingredients.
- ♦ Cover and chill for 1 hour.
- ♦ Preheat oven to 375°
- ♦ Combine ¼ cup sugar and 1 Tbls. cinnamon in bowl.
- ♦ Shape dough into 1 inch balls. Roll in cinnamon and sugar mixture.
- ♦ Please on ungreased cookie sheet.
- ♦ Bake about 10 minutes.

# OATMEAL COOKIES

1½ sticks butter
1 cup brown sugar
½ cup sugar
1 egg
1½ cups flour
1 teaspoon baking powder
1 teaspoon vanilla

1 teaspoon cinnamon
½ teaspoon cloves
½ teaspoon nutmeg
½ teaspoon ginger
2 cups rolled oats
1 cup raisins

- ♦ Preheat oven to 375°
- ♦ In a bowl cream butter and sugar. Add other ingredients.
- ♦ Drop dough by teaspoonfuls on cookie sheet.
- ♦ Bake 10-12 minutes.

# PEANUT CHOCOLATE COOKIES

2 sticks butter
2 cups sugar
2 eggs
2 teaspoons vanilla

2 cups flour
1 cup peanut chips
1 cup chocolate chips

- ♦ Preheat oven to 375°
- ♦ Cream butter and sugar. Add other ingredients.
- ♦ Drop by teaspoonful onto ungreased cookie sheet.
- ♦ Bake 8-10 minutes.

# CHOCOLATE DIAMONDS

2 squares unsweetened
chocolate
1 stick butter
1 cup sugar
2 eggs

½ cup flour
¼ teaspoon sugar
½ teaspoon vanilla
¾ cup nuts

- ♦ Preheat oven to 400°
- ♦ Melt the chocolate and butter in sauce pan. Remove from heat and add rest of ingredients.
- ♦ Drop by teaspoons onto cookie sheet
- ♦ Bake 12 minutes.

# RUM BALLS

2¼ cups ginger snaps
1 cup pecans
¼ cup cocoa

1 cup powdered sugar
¼ cup Karo syrup
¼ cup dark rum

- ♦ Combine all ingredients in food processor.
- ♦ Roll into balls.
- ♦ Roll in cocoa or powdered sugar.

# HERBS AND SPICES

McCormick & Company, Inc. in Baltimore is the world's largest provider of spices. The company was founded in 1889 by Willoughby M. McCormick. The first products were sold under the "Bee Brand" and "Silver Medal" brand. Today McCormick produces a number of different products including Old Bay Seasoning. Wye Island Seasoning is also very popular.

There are a number of herbs and spices found in the Chesapeake region. Not only are they used in cooking, but even the Native Americans found medicinal uses that have been passed on to present generations. Among these are:

Mint is an aromatic herb used to flavor tea, vegetables, cold drinks, fruits, salads, lamb, candies, jellies, and desserts. Did you know that it can also repel insects and mice?

Thyme is a member of the mint family and is used to season soups, poultry, fish, cheese and flavor Benedictine liqueur. Its medicinal properties have been known since ancient times.

Rosemary is also a member of the mint family and is a symbol of remembrance, affection, fidelity or constancy. Greek Students once wore garlands of rosemary in their hair while taking examinations as they thought it increased memory. The early colonists used it to scent soap. Today it is used on roasts and roasting potatoes and other vegetables.

Rosemary is a strong, resinous flavoring for lamb, beef, chicken and other dishes. In early times it was used to mask odors on especially gamy meats. During the holidays rosemary wreathes and trees are popular decorations.

Parsley was brought to the colonies by early settlers and is used to garnish and flavor various dishes. Among these are bouquet garni, sauces, salads, stews, and vegetables.

Chervil is an aromatic herb similar to parsley and a member of the carrot family. It is most often used in soups and salads.

Sage is also a member of the mint family used to flavor meats and chicken, and is known for its healing powers.

Basil, also a member of the mint family, was called the "Herb of Kings" in Greece. It is used with soups, cheese, pastas, salads, eggs, fish, stuffings, tomatoes, and pesto.

Tarragon is a member of the aster family and is used especially in vinegar, mayonnaise, on poultry, salads, eggs and many other dishes.

Dill is a member of the parsley family. It is used for seasoning soups, salads, pickles, vegetable, egg, fish, poultry dishes and breads. Both dill weed and seed are used.

Lavender is mainly used in dried bouquets, but can also flavor meats and teas. The word comes from lavare "to wash". It has also has medicinal uses.

Lavender is most often thought of as a potpourri for linens, but it can also be used in cakes, cookies, muffins, teas, jellies and vinegar.

Chives are milder than onions with a long green stem. They are used in soups, salads, omelets, cottage cheese, potato and egg dishes.

Marjoram is a member of the mint family. Its leaves are used in soups, salads, and with chicken and lamb.

Oregano is wild marjoram and is used in many Italian dishes, especially to flavor tomato dishes and sauces.

Mustard seeds are used for pickling, in sauerkraut and salads, such as coleslaw.

Bay leaf can be added to stews, soups, tomatoes, or in meat pies.

Garlic can reduce cholesterol levels and can be used as an antibiotic, anti-cancer and cardiovascular treatment. Garlic can be used in meat, potato, salad and vegetable dishes.

Thyme has been called the "blending herb" and can be used in variety of dishes. These include soups, salads, stews, chicken and egg dishes, cheese and with vegetables.

# Index

241

# ABOUT THE AUTHOR

Katie Barney Moose, born in Baltimore, is a descendant of old New England whaling families and the Clagett (Claggett) family of Maryland. She has lived in many of the U.S.' great culinary, architectural, historical and waterside gems- New Castle, DE; Newport and Providence, RI; Cold Spring Harbor, NY; San Francisco; Philadelphia; Greenwich, CT; Alexandria, VA; Washington, DC; Annapolis, MD and New York City. She presently resides in Easton, MD.

Mrs. Moose is in the process of publishing a series of regional cookbooks, and guidebooks on the different regions of the Chesapeake Bay and cookbooks on New England. She has also published "Uniquely Delaware" and "Uniquely Rhode Island" for Heinemann Publishers of New York. She was the co-author of "The Best of Newport, the Newport Guidebook", several publications on the fiber optic telecommunications business, and is a consultant on international business and protocol. Her hobbies beside gourmet cooking and fine wine, include history, sailing, genealogy, theology and travel.

# ORDER FORM FOR CONDUIT PRESS BOOKS

Please send me _____ copies of Chesapeake's Bounty II @ $17.95

Please send me _____ copies of New England's Bounty @ $17.95

Please send me _____ copies of Nantucket's Bounty @ $17.95

Please send me _____ copies of Chesapeake's Bounty @ $16.95

Please send me _____ copies of Maryland's Western Shore: The Guidebook @ $15.95

Please send me _____ copies of Eastern Shore of Maryland: The Guidebook @ $16.95

Add postage for 1$^{st}$ book @ $4.00 _____
Postage for each additional book @ $1.00 _____
Gift wrap per book @ $2.00 _____
Total order _____

❑ Check or money order enclosed
❑ Make payable to Conduit Press

Mail to: Conduit Press
307 Goldsborough Street
Easton, MD 21601

Ship books to:

Name_____

Address_____

_____

Telephone_____

For further information please
• Call 410-820-9915
• E-mail: kamoose@erols.com

# NOTES